7 Laws of Highest Prosperity

Making your life count
for what really counts!

7 Laws of Highest Prosperity

Cecil O. Kemp Jr.
with Kathryn Knight

MANJUL
Manjul Publishing House

First published in India by

MANJUL

Manjul Publishing House Pvt. Ltd.

Corporate Office:
2nd Floor, Usha Preet Complex,
42 Malviya Nagar, Bhopal 462 003 - India
E-mail: manjul@manjulindia.com Website: www.manjulindia.com

Marketing Office:
7/32, Ground Floor, Ansari Road, Daryaganj, New Delhi 110 002
Email: booksupplyco@gmail.com

This edition first published in 2005
Third impression 2012

Warning: If financial advice or assistance is required, the services of a competent professional should be sought. The author and publisher have not written or sold this publication representing or intending it to be financial or investment advice.

ISBN 978 - 81 - 8322 - 113 - 9

Printed & bound in India by Manipal Technologies Ltd., Manipal.

I dedicate this book to my parents.

From them I learned some of life's most valuable lessons.
More importantly, they first pointed me to Divine Wisdom
as the best answer for life's many questions.

The lyrics of Steve Wariner's country hit song "Holes in the Floor of Heaven" express my emotional and spiritual journey since my dad's unexpected death in 1995.
Cecil Sr., I feel your tears of joy and pride coming through the holes in the floor of heaven as you watch over me.
It was your life, your example, your love, and your death that inspired me to write.

Thank you and your beloved wife, my mother, Peggy,
for the honor and privilege of being your son.

Contents

Acknowledgments

My highest praise and thanks go to the heavenly Father.

To the reader, thank you for buying this book. My hopes and prayers are that it inspires and encourages you, empowering you to make wise, honorable, and hopeful decisions with your life and money.

Thanks, for all your prayers and encouragement, to my wife, Patty; our children and their spouses, Heather and Chris and Rusty and Tracy; Ms. Clara Millican of Decaturville, Tennessee; Ms. Dora Medaris of Birmingham, Alabama; and many, many others.

Thanks to our grandchildren, Briley, Jessi, and Justus (and those still to be!) for restoring to me life's wonder, joy, and passion.

Thanks to Wes Yoder and Ron Miller of Ambassador Agency and many other creative individuals who stood with Patty and me and believed in this book and, along the way, made unique and very valuable contributions.

Thanks to Diana Donovan, Celo Valley Books in Burnsville, North Carolina, for creating the interior design and layout and for editing the manuscript; and to Natalie Cox Jaynes, Monica Hall, and all those you worked with at Anderson-Thomas Design in Nashville, for the cover design and back cover text. All your contributions made a big difference!

Last but certainly not least, deep and heartfelt thanks to my writing associate, Kathryn Knight. You are a very special person, an extraordinarily enlightened, insightful, and passionate soul who shares my life philosophy and values. I know your editing and writing skills and wise, honorable, and hopeful heart will come through clearly to readers. This book is as much from your heart as it is from mine.

Foreword

In 1923 a very important meeting took place in Chicago. Of this high-powered group of people who knew the secrets of making money, nine were the most financially successful people in the world at that time.

Where were these nine twenty-five years later, in 1948?

Six of them had known how to make a lot of money but had failed to truly prosper because they didn't live by the 7 Laws of Highest Prosperity. By 1948 a great wheat speculator had died abroad, insolvent. A president of the largest independent steel company had died bankrupt after living on borrowed money for the five previous years. A president of a large utility company had died a fugitive from justice, penniless in a foreign land. A member of the President's Cabinet had been pardoned from prison only to die at home shortly thereafter. A president of the New York Stock Exchange was in prison. A president of a successful gas company was insane.

The other three *did* live by those laws, and they remained not merely wealthy but genuinely prosperous, like many of history's happiest and most successful people who have pursued prosperity (not simply material wealth).

Dive in and let Sam the wood gatherer teach you about life and material resources!

The authors hope that when you emerge—like the three mentioned above who succeeded and like Sam the wood gatherer—you will choose to take the journey to highest prosperity.

Apply the 7 Laws of Highest Prosperity and make your life count for what really counts!

1

The Restless Voice

The wood gatherer was a young man—a rather simple man who came from a family of wood gatherers who, in turn, came from families of wood gatherers. Good people with a simple approach to life. People who worked very hard at maintaining their station in life—for this is very hard work indeed to maintain one's station, is it not?

And perhaps that is why the village folk found it odd that Sam—our simple wood gatherer—was a questioning sort of young man. "Why do the lords of the realm live in great houses made of brick? And why do we gather wood all day from the forest floors to sell to the townsfolk—yet have so little left to fuel our own fires? Why is there so little joy in our lives, even though we work very hard and dedicate ourselves to our tasks?"

Not one in the village could answer young Sam's persistent questions. One woman, bent double from carrying bundles of wood all her life, growled, "The lords live in great homes because they have wealth! We are not destined to have wealth! We are destined to keep to ourselves and be happy with what we have."

"But you're not happy, Magda," replied Sam. "You groan under each load and envy the townsfolk for the delicious fruits they eat and their music festivals and dancing. . . ."

"I am very happy!" snapped Magda. "I know my place and can live just fine without the apples and pears and music of the town." And she returned to her work—grumbling.

And so, young Sam resumed his wood gathering every day, trying to ignore the doubts, curiosity, and longing of his own heart . . .

until one day . . .

. . . when the town buyer of wood became ill and could not bring his cart to the forest village. Several young men from the village—including Sam—were sent on the long trek through the forest to the town square, their backs laden with bundles of wood. The walk was arduous, and Sam could not help but wonder why the village did not own a cart of its own.

The town square was bustling with activity. The humble village men stood to one side, waiting for someone to come buy their wood. Instead the merchants gathered around others in the square. Brick sellers, paper sellers, fruit sellers, wheat sellers—who were all happily extolling the excellence of their products.

Taking note, young Sam spoke up. "If anyone needs good firewood, find it here—the very best from the forest."

The other village men stared at Sam in astonishment. "Hush!" warned one man. "We are merely poor folk who offer twigs and branches. Show not pride, for we are but humble village dwellers—"

But he was interrupted by a well-dressed gentleman in green woolen clothes who stepped over and asked young Sam the price of his wood.

"We receive two farthings a cord from the buyer who visits our village. This is the price we offer you."

"Two farthings? What a bargain for the very best firewood. I'll buy the lot."

And so the forest dwellers returned home, happy with their sale but weary from the journey. They were so weary, they gathered very little the next day and so had very little to carry to the town—which trip was still necessary, as the town buyer was not yet well enough to travel.

Again they stood in the town square, and again young Sam called out, "If anyone needs good firewood, find it here—the very best from the forest."

Promptly, the same gentleman in the sporty green woolen clothes stepped over. But this time he took young Sam aside and spoke to him in a soft voice.

"I will buy all your wood again at two farthings a cord, but I know why it is so cheap. Other firewood sells for six farthings a cord—more pricey—but it burns well into the night. This wood is partly rotted and quite old indeed, from having been on the forest floor so long, yes? It will burn, but very quickly and with much smoke. Tell me, do you not find it so in your own fires?"

Sam thought for a moment. "Yes. It burns much too quickly. We are constantly feeding our fires to keep warm. This keeps our fire tenders busy all day and night."

"So you agree this is not the best firewood from the forest."

"Perhaps not," replied Sam, "but we work so very, very hard all day . . ."

"But you agree this is not the very best firewood from the forest."

Sam spoke quietly. "I guess I do agree."

The man, as he promised, bought every bit of wood, which amounted to just enough money for bread and which relieved the men of their loads for their return home. Yet all the way back, Sam wondered why he felt so burdened. . . .

2

The Determined Heart

Sam returned to the village with a heavy heart, but said nothing that evening to his family or fellow villagers. Instead he mulled over the words of the gentleman with the warm green woolen clothes.

The next morning as the men and women were bent upon their daily tasks, Sam decided to engage his gathering companion in conversation.

"We always gather the easiest wood to find and carry, yes?"

"Of course."

"And why is that so?"

"Because it has always been so. Our work is so laborious that we would be foolish to go farther than necessary to find wood or to carry the largest pieces of fallen wood in the forest. How our backs would ache then!"

"But we remain so poor. Perhaps we are poor because we offer poor wood," suggested Sam.

His companion stopped and glared at Sam. "Are you insulting the hard work we do in this village?"

"I simply—"

"Are you demeaning our efforts?" demanded his fellow villager.

"No, no. Not at all," said Sam. "I was just thinking that our great efforts could be put to better use. Perhaps we can—"

"Perhaps we can stop talking nonsense and continue our work. Who are we to question the ways that have always been? Do we not have just enough to buy bread from the town bread man? Does he not bring enough each day in his cart to our village? Do we not have shelter in our twig-and-mud huts? Do we not have each other to share in our . . . in our . . ."

"Misery?" offered Sam.

The fellow wood gatherer stood up straight—as straight as his crooked back would allow—and stared angrily off into the trees. "We may be poor. We may even be miserable. But we are a village and I am proud of my work. My exhaustion at the end of the day is a mark of my contribution to my family and village. You would do best to take pride in your work, young man. Leave me now to my work."

Sam stood and thought for a long time. He thought about what this wood gatherer had said. He thought about what the townsman had said. He thought about what his heart said. . . .

"I will," he then said to himself. "From this day on, I will take pride in my work."

At midday, the gatherers brought their day's work to the village center. Stacks and stacks of twigs and branches formed a large pile, to be divvied out to the men who would take it to town. The pile was not as large as usual, since the gatherers were worn out from the walk to town each day, but surely, they thought, this would still buy enough bread for the evening meal.

A joyful whistling coming from the forest turned all the villagers' heads. Into the clearing came Sam, laden with a few large branches—and even two cracked oak logs. He laid them at the edge of the pile, smiling.

"You fool," cried a villager. "You have gathered fewer pieces than all the others. You have been lazy in your work."

Still smiling, Sam responded, "No, good woman, I have not been lazy. I have brought the very best wood I could find, and this means I traveled through the forest until I found what

I was looking for—a windbreak not far from King's new road, which he built a few years ago. See these fine pieces! They will burn well! I have worked hard and traveled far and my legs are quite weary indeed!"

"But you were . . . whistling!" accused another.

Sam nodded. "My legs are weary but my heart is light, for I know that today I have done my very best and can offer the very best."

The others knew not how to respond. Muttering, they went straight to the task of loading up the men who would walk to town. Sam elected to take his entire load—which, amazingly, he carried all the way to town without a groan.

Nor did he gloat with self-satisfaction as the men returned to the village. Although his heart was happy indeed from having watched the gentleman with the green woolen clothes hand over six farthings for his load of very fine wood, he did not smirk at his fellow villagers. And although his heart swelled with pride when he handed the six farthings to the bread man the next day for extra bread for himself and the village, he did not point this out to anyone. Instead he attended to his work diligently, always whistling, and always happy . . .

until one day . . .

. . . when the recovered town wood buyer was able to once again bring his cart to the forest village to purchase and transport the firewood. The village was delighted, to say the least, for their efforts had been sorely diminished by their weary daily walks to town. Had it not been for Sam's six farthings each day, many of the villagers would have gone hungry.

In fact, everyone was relieved . . . except Sam, who had come to relish the sights and sounds of the activity of the town. He loved to see the bright faces of the potters, the apple sellers, the mothers and their plump, healthy children. He took in every detail—the sturdy homes made of fine split logs and sun-baked bricks, the clean, warm clothing of the wealthiest townspeople—dyed green, blue, red, yellow. . . . This view of what he took to be prosperity amazed young Sam and made his hard-won load of wood barely noticeable as he anticipated each visit.

But now there were no walks to town. Instead there were many more hours for gathering, gathering, and more gathering. And although Sam was proud to continue to gather at the spot where he had found the long-dead trees leaning against each other, off the ground, proud of his new agility from working his way along hanging limbs to harvest his branches, proud of his sharpened eye that could spot pieces of limb that had fallen and cracked but not yet dampened, proud to offer his fine wood each day to the wood buyer, he still longed for more satisfaction in life.

And that is how—although at the time, Sam had no idea of what was coming— Sam's long, long hours of wood gathering came to be put to the very best use of all. For it was during these long days of longing . . . that Sam began to dream. . . .

3

Let the Dreams Begin!

The long, tedious days of a wood gatherer rarely held meaning. Every day ran into the next with a numbing monotony and boredom that could rob the soul, mind, and body of joy, beauty, and hope. And because this was so, the villagers explained away their flat, steady existence with a self-imposed resignation that this was how their lives were meant to be. To dare to think that they could better their lot was an admission of failure. Did they not have enough bread? Did they not serve a purpose—albeit insignificant—to clear the rotted wood and supply the town with a cheap source of fuel? Surely they were better off than the beggars in town, or the wealthy land barons who must be terribly lonely and unhappy with all their gold. . . .

And so, faithfully each evening, the villagers silently, by rote, prayed, "Thank you" to God for providing the wood that sustained their meager lives.

But Sam prayed a bit differently. "Thank you, God, for giving me the strength to carry this hard-won wood back to the village, for it brings more money that benefits us all."

And Sam's days were a bit different too. Each day he returned whistling. And each morning he arose eager to work, for the forest offered more than wood. It offered solace, and quiet time to truly listen to the sounds around him and the dreams of his heart.

All day he "daydreamed" about saving a wee bit from his earnings until he could buy a cart. How grand that would be! For with a cart, two men could haul the wood to town each day—and surely the wood buyer would pay the village a bit extra if they delivered the wood to him! And with this same cart, the bread could be hauled back to the village—and surely the bread man would charge a bit less if he also did not have to travel to the village. . . . And perhaps—perhaps there would be others who would be willing to gather the better wood with him, and the village could earn enough for fresh fruit. . . . And perhaps the village could even work fewer hours and spend some evenings singing—maybe dancing!—around a community campfire . . . with smiles on their faces and happy children . . . listening. . . .

Sam loved his days—his endless, exhausting days of hard work and spirited dreams.

But when he shared his thoughts with fellow villagers, he got blank stares or disdainful looks in return.

"You have time to spend your days dreaming?"

"A cart, he says! A cart that will need mending! A cart that will get stuck in mud on rainy days! Let the townsmen bother with carts—let them deal with the problems of owning them—let *them* come to *us*."

"You want the rest of us to go farther for wood and learn to shinny up trunks to get branches when we can gather branches from the forest floor? What if we fall and break our backs?"

"No, no," Sam responded as calmly as he could. "You won't fall. I'll show some younger ones how to break the branches off, others can hold their ankles so they don't fall, and the older ones can untangle the branches thrown down and sort them for carrying to the village. We could get a good supply in a little less time if we work together like that. And though the distance is more, the weight of the wood is less, since it is drier than what you've been gathering. If all our wood were that dry and solid, the town buyer would pay more for it because it's wood the townsfolk truly want. . . ."

"*Townsfolk* want! *They* want! All you seem to care about is what *they* want! Are you their servant? If you take the wood to them each day, they'll not be grateful—they'll not pay more."

"First you gather the wood *they* want. . . . Now you want us to do that too, and you even want to deliver it *to* them! Are you a villager or a townsman?"

"Are we not already bound together in some way . . . ?" started Sam.

"*You* are bound to *them.* They care nothing for us. They see us as poor, groveling wood gatherers who mean nothing. Why should we bend over backward to please them?"

Sam turned back to his work, silently, thinking, "Because they *see* us as poor groveling wood gatherers who are worth nothing to them."

And so it was that Sam endured his wood-gathering days, with his dreams and hopes locked inside him. But his heart brimmed with inspiration and his eyes were filled with visions of a better life—a happier life that would be more of a celebration than a drudgery . . .

until one day . . .

. . . when Sam was suddenly struck with an idea that seemed to come to him during a moment of divine inspiration. He had been praying earnestly, wistfully, as he searched, slid out to the ends of limbs, gathered what he dropped to the ground, and then stacked his branches for carrying back to the village. "God, creator of all the wonder in this forest: Surely you wish more happiness for your children. Yet we seem to be stuck in the worst possible life—for what could be worse than thanklessly gathering wood all day, living in poverty with no joy? And what could be worse than endlessly yearning for a better life for myself and my fellow villagers, only to be scoffed at by the others? What could be worse?" he implored.

And then it hit him with such truth and such weight that he stood stunned, dropping a fine piece of wood.

There was indeed something worse than poverty. There was something worse than ridicule. There was something infinitely worse. It was to dream—to listen to his own heart while it communed with the Divine Spirit—and then do nothing. It was to listen to men who knew not—instead of listening to God and his own honorable heart.

In that one moment Sam realized that his life would not—could not—be contained in his forest village. Something better awaited him, and the only other "out there" he knew of was the town.

The next day Sam did something no villager had done in recent memory. He packed up a bundle of clothes and loaded his back with the biggest load of fine wood he could bear, and he lovingly bade farewell to his fellow villagers. And with a song in his heart and a vision in his mind, he walked the long path to town.

4

Building . . . Wealth?

So it was that Sam became a townsman. He arrived with wood, earned eight farthings, and inquired of the gentleman in the fine green wool coat where he might find suitable lodgings and work for day wages.

Because Sam had already proven himself to be an honest man, the gentleman in the green wool coat recommended him to a foreman in charge of building homes in the town. The gentleman also prepared a comfortable place in his stables for Sam to stay until he had earned enough to situate himself elsewhere.

Sam's duties for the foreman Grecco included helping to haul large felled trees to be cut into timber for building. Sam was grateful and felt truly blessed to be of service—to earn his keep and apply the little knowledge he knew about wood gathering. He worked diligently, honestly—whistling through the day, sleeping soundly at night—and soon saved enough to sign a lease for a small, comfortable room above the head mason's carriage house.

Sam learned all he could from his fellow workers, and his keen sense of observation and reasoning impressed not only his crew, but the foreman as well. Sam devised a strong cart with two wheels, which he gave the use of to his crew; it allowed several logs to be hauled by fewer men. He encouraged the planting of new trees to replace the ones they felled, showing foresight and concern for the next generations. He also worked, after hours, without pay, to help those in the town less fortunate to build small wood-and-mud huts of their own.

The foreman naturally noticed this valuable worker, and within a year asked him to work with his framing crew on the larger homes and business establishments in the town.

"Sir," responded Sam, "I think it only fair to let you know I have only built huts. I truly know nothing about actual framing, stonework, or masonry. I would be eager to apprentice, but—"

"You will be perfect!" announced Grecco. "Since you know nothing, you will learn everything the correct way from the beginning. Come, let's get you started!"

And so they did.

Sam was grateful, earnest, happy, and hopeful about his future. His eyes were opened to a whole new line of work, and also to a whole new way of life. He was in awe of the grand homes and buildings that began to take shape—in part because of his own efforts. The huts on the far outskirts of the town seemed miles away in his mind. The huts even farther away, in the forest village, were only a vague memory—of a life past, a dim dream. . . .

Now a member of this large and bustling town, Sam courted and married the finest seamstress in the town, Suzette—a woman who both loved and admired Sam—and for this again he felt truly blessed. He took her back to his meager room above the mason's carriage house and promised her that within two years they would have a home of their own. Together they dreamed about and planned for their home—a cozy cottage in the market area, with a room in front with a big window where Suzette could sew, embroider, and welcome customers. Together they dreamed of a family and a comfortable, warm place with lovely things to lift their spirits and fine books and food to feed their souls and bodies. Sam had never felt so fortunate—nor so prosperous—in all his life!

But there are two seemingly contradictory things that tend to be true for the human race. One is that people can get used to anything: They can live in the lowliest or the most inhumane conditions and somehow reduce their expectations and hopes in order to survive with just a small fraction of soul-spark intact. The other thing about people is that no matter how blessed their lives may be, there is a tendency to want more—simply for "more's" sake—to have what the more wealthy man has, and then to have what the very wealthiest man has. It's a "me too" voice that sneaks into the corners of the mind and clouds out the clear, quieter, more profound voice of divine inspiration, celebration, and truth.

And Sam was quite human. (Yes, he may seem so moral and cheerful and honorable that he could hardly be a real human being, but real he was.) And into his mind crept the "me too" voice—so slowly and insidiously that neither he nor Suzette could even sense the transition until it had taken Sam down a detour that led to a roadblock of debt, wants, defenses, and misery.

It began when one of Sam's fellow crewmen purchased a small home—a worker who earned a bit less than Sam but who could rely on financial help from his parents and brother. Sam was smitten with the desire to own a house—*now.* And despite Suzette's concerns, he took out a loan for a house that stretched their budget and required longer hours at work.

Fortunately, his excellent work earned him a promotion to foreman—which delighted him, eased his financial burden and gave him the authority to instruct his crew to build with integrity, attention to detail, and efficiency. His crew was in demand all over the town and even in neighboring towns.

. . .

Eleven years after Sam had come to town and six after he became a foreman, he and Suzette had three children, but Sam was rarely home to truly enjoy either them or his cozy home. Sam took every job offered and worked himself and his crew day and night. Sam's wealth had indeed grown, but so had his appetites. When the chief foreman Grecco showed up in a new suit, Sam ordered himself such a suit the very next day. When the mayor rode through town in his black carriage, Sam at first vowed to own one like it within three years—but he borrowed to purchase one only six months later. Sam cultivated acquaintances with wealthy townsmen and learned that they invested in other businesses besides their own. He felt unknowledgeable and insecure, yet motivated and ambitious—all at the same time. He knew he was a good worker, a smart man, and he was certain that he was entitled to whatever any other man had!

Suzette's days consisted of attending to her children and her limited but steady work as a seamstress. With growing anxiety, she watched her admirable Sam grow more agitated, distant, and self-serving each day. He didn't whistle anymore. His crewman no longer enjoyed his instruction—or rather commands—and some left him to earn less pay on other crews. When Sam came home one day and announced that they were moving into a grand brick home on Miller Street, Suzette wasn't sure if she felt happy or bewildered. How could they afford such a home? she wisely inquired. "How can we afford not to?" was Sam's reply. "Surely the best foreman in the town should look successful—I can't live in this small house! If I'm going to be prosperous, I need to look successful."

And where did Sam get that idea? Surely not from the voice that had at one time spoken to him in the quiet of a forest. . . .

Sam did indeed look prosperous—but his mounting bills made him more anxious about every contract that came his way. He hurried his crews in order to start new projects. He ignored the pleadings of his best workers and of his beloved wife to stop and think about his decisions. He took advice from shifty businessmen and lost money on poor investments. His contracts suffered, his home suffered, his mind suffered, and his business dropped off.

A year after his move to Miller Street, Sam found himself on the brink of financial ruin, with only one contract left and time instead of money on his hands. Financial failure consumed his every thought. To Sam, financial failure meant complete failure—period. The prosperity he had lost was what meant everything. Sam knew—he just knew—that if he could get one more loan, he could tide himself over until he regained his business . . . and then he and his family would be happy . . . once more. . . .

These were the thoughts that filled his self-pitying, desperate mind as he denied to himself that his own choices had led him to such a sorry state . . .

until one day . . .

. . . when he was approached on the street by a fine older gentleman who jauntily asked of him, "Why . . . aren't you Sam, the wood gatherer from the village? You are doing well, I assume?"

"Very well," replied Sam, though his voice and expression could not mask his misery.

The older gentlemen studied his face. "But you are not happy, my man. I remember always thinking what a happy young man you were. Are you ill? Is anyone in your family ill?"

A bit aggravated, Sam responded with impatience, "No one is ill. My family does well, despite my recent business failures; I am but between successes. I have determined to become the most prosperous man in the town, and nothing—and no one—will keep me from attaining all I deserve." Sam was taken by surprise at how easily he had revealed such a personal ambition to this man.

The older gentlemen kept studying Sam, now with an even keener eye. "You wish highest prosperity, Sam?"

"Of course—doesn't everyone?"

"I suppose so," replied the gentleman. He reflected for a moment before adding, "But not all seem to claim it."

"Claim it? You mean earn it! And what do you know about prosperity anyway? Your clothes look rather plain to me.

A-a-and . . . ," stuttered Sam out of embarrassment and bewilderment, "and why am I talking to you of such things?"

"Because I know how to help you," replied the gentleman with quiet authority, never shifting his eyes from Sam's face.

Caught off guard, Sam demanded, "How do you know? And . . . how do you know my name?"

"I am Menro—the man who first bought your wood. The man who first directed you to the foreman Grecco. I put you up in my stables for your first weeks in town."

Sam was stunned. Menro—the gentleman who usually wore the green wool coat. "And you remember me after all these years?"

"But of course, my man. You used to whistle while you carried your load of fine wood!" Menro's eyes twinkled. "I always knew you were destined for a happy life."

"Happy! I have no time for happiness—not yet. Only when I can see my family in the largest house in town . . . when I own the finest horses and commission the best gardeners to tend my orchards . . . only then will I be happy. I must redeem myself, for I have become a failure. In fact, I'm on my way to Geoffrey the moneylender. If I can but buy some fine things now, I will find a way to pay for them and—"

"Ah, you are truly in earnest," Menro said gently. Then he paused before adding, "I can help you. . . ."

Sam was cautious. How many times had he heard business associates, customers, and vendors say "I can help you" only to learn they were bent on helping their own interests?

"Are you friends with the moneylender?" Sam inquired warily.

"Not friends, no. But I know of someone who knows his dealings inside out and can advise you in all matters of success. In fact, if anyone can help you realize your goal of highest prosperity, I believe Magowin can. Yes, yes. . . . In fact the more I think of it, you really must stop by and visit him. You cannot miss his shop—he's the shoemaker on Dairy Street—just three shops from the moneylender's. . . ."

Sam's pent-up anxieties, hopes, and desperation burst out

in a fit of laughter—a sad, gasping laughter that revealed a soul without peace. "A cobbler! Oh, yes, Menro," Sam retorted sarcastically. "I certainly will go to the cobbler—surely he is a man of great fortune who can advise me in all matters of financial prosperity!"

"I know you will, Sam. I know you will." Patting Sam firmly on the shoulder as he moved past him, Menro went on his way down the cobblestone street.

"Now I'm late!" muttered Sam, and he turned onto Dairy Street, passed the shoemaker's shop, and made his way to Geoffrey the moneylender's door—where hung a sign that read: CLOSED EARLY FOR THE DAY.

Now what? After a few minutes of frustration, during which Sam angrily blamed the moneylender for all his own problems, Sam determined that he would find the moneylender and plead his case. But where to start? Then he remembered the old gentleman's words: *But I know of someone who knows his dealings inside out. . . .* Magowin the cobbler! Magowin might know where Geoffrey had gone!

And so it was that Sam found himself at the door of a humble cobbler who, by the way, was whistling a merry tune as Sam entered the shop. . . .

5

Sole Searching

"Come in, my good man! Ah, you look like a man whose soles need mending, yes?"

Sam looked across a wooden bench strewn with every sort of foot apparel imaginable—from sandals to leather work boots, from elegant beaded dancing shoes to carved wooden clogs—and then into the azure-blue eyes of a whiskered, bespectacled, smiling, pleasant old cobbler.

"Er, no." Sam began, then felt a bit self-conscious. If Magowin did know the moneylender well, Sam had better be polite. "No, sir," he said more brightly. "Actually I'm here to see if you might know where I could find Geoffrey the moneylender. You see, it's terribly important that I talk to him today. . . . It concerns . . . it concerns a cousin of mine who is in sad straits. You see—" Sam cleared his throat. "So you see, I need to find him, and Menro suggested that you could help me."

"Ah, Menro!" Magowin leaned his head back and laughed heartily. "A man who stays with the same pair of shoes for ten years! Can you imagine? For ten years? Not good for my business, no, but we are good friends. Yes, good friends." The cobbler put down the pink leather slipper he was working on and looked squarely into Sam's worry-lined face. "But you don't care about that, young man, no. Come, sit over here and tell why you seek this moneylender."

Feeling out of place but having nowhere else to turn, Sam sidled over to the vacant chair and found that he was relieved to sink into it. The cobbler's shop was pleasant indeed, in a warm, safe sort of way. It smelled of leather and wood shavings and perhaps a hint of fresh-baked bread. "So, you do know where he is?" asked Sam in earnest.

"I know. Yes, I know. And you're right—I know him quite well. We have had discussions, many discussions, and . . . well, I've taught him quite a bit about financial strategy."

"You?" Sam quickly realized that his comment was out of line. "What I mean, sir, is that—"

"It's quite all right, my good man. Quite all right. But you see, though I earn my living making shoes and mending soles, I live by a set of laws that can be taught to any person—and I have taught many men and women who were willing to listen to my words as well as to their own hearts. You might say I'm in the happiness business."

Sam leaned forward. "What do you teach?"

"How to attain highest prosperity." The cobbler casually reached into his pocket, pulled out two ripe plums, and handed one to Sam. "Care to join me?"

In all his days, Sam could not remember a more strange encounter—a more odd moment, a more curious circumstance—than this. Sitting in a small cobbler shop in a comfortable chair, biting into a plum, wondering what he was supposed to say and forgetting why he was there in the first place. . . . There was something very unreal about the whole picture, yet something very real and familiar. . . .

Then Sam felt himself snap out of it and he responded to Magowin. "Highest prosperity? What do you mean you teach how to attain it? *Where* do you teach? Are you a wealthy man?"

"Hmm. Some would say so," said Magowin, casually picking up the pink leather slipper. "Where do I teach? I teach in my shop, I teach on the street, I teach wherever I meet my students. Are you looking for a teacher?" Magowin started working intently on the slipper.

Sam squirmed in his chair, uncomfortable now. "No. I'm looking for Geoffrey the moneylender."

"Why, my good man?"

Magowin's voice was so sincere and warm that Sam found himself saying, "I need to borrow money so that my family and I can stay in our home. It's just until I get my business going again—temporarily, you know. Actually"—Sam faked a little chuckle—"actually I'm a prosperous man, myself. Times are just a bit hard right now. I was misled into some bad investments and other foremen took my best crewmen. I've had picky clients and demanding vendors and workers who don't work fast enough. But things will change. . . ."

"Yes, I see," replied Magowin calmly, still working on the slipper. "Well, I'm so glad you're a prosperous man because I only teach prosperous people."

Sam did a quick double take. "What do you mean you only teach prosperous people? Why do you teach them if they're already prosperous?" Sam found he was no longer at ease in the cobbler's shop, and he got out of his chair to leave. "Anyway, I don't need a teacher. I know very well how to become successful financially. I did it once, I can do it again. I came here looking for the moneylender. He's the one I need."

Magowin put the slipper down, stood, turned to this searching, lost man, and spoke words that Sam would never, ever forget as long as he lived.

"No, Sam. You don't need the moneylender. He won't help you now. You owe him too much already and he has no desire to see you fall into ruin. What you need you already have—you must simply trust and claim it. What you need is to celebrate the prosperity that already belongs to you. What you need is to rediscover how to whistle. What you need is to understand what true success is all about. What you need, Sam, is to learn and follow the laws that lead to contentment, fulfillment, and highest prosperity."

Sam was stunned. He stood, mouth agape, staring at this odd little whiskered man who had just been working on a pink slipper. Sam found himself asking, "Will you teach me?"

"But of course!" Magowin slapped his visitor on the back and laughed heartily. "Thought you'd never ask! Come back tomorrow at two o'clock! We'll begin—and while we talk you can help me with my work. Fair enough?" Magowin walked Sam to the door, his hand resting on the younger man's shoulder.

Again Sam found himself answering as if he himself were not really speaking. "Yes. Two o'clock. I'll be here."

"Wonderful! Oh, but one more thing. Before we meet, I want you to review your entire life. Answer these questions" —For emphasis, Magowin held up a new finger for each question—"How did your family make a living? What did they teach you about money? What makes you happy when you work?—Let's see now. . . . Oh, yes!—What attracted you to your wife? What goes through your head when you think about work, saving, giving, spending? Prioritize your needs.

"And then prioritize your values," Magowin continued, as though this "one more thing" were a simple assignment. "Ask yourself: What values did you learn as a child that have affected your views on money and success? What values do you intend to teach your children? How much do you include your wife in financial decision making? How do you define success? What's the source of your contentment? What's the source of your discontentment? What are your good habits and what are your bad habits? And . . ." Magowin peered at Sam over his tiny spectacles. "And who are you really, Sam, and why do you want to be prosperous?"

"Wait, wait!" cried Sam, overwhelmed with this deluge. "I'll be up all night if I try to answer all those questions!"

"What a wonderful answer!" exclaimed Magowin with great joy. "I'm so glad you didn't say that this can't be done at all!" He embraced Sam lightly, then returned to his work, and added as a side note, "You had best get started, then! See you at two o'clock tomorrow."

Sam was halfway home when it occurred to him that he had never told Magowin his name, yet obviously, somehow the old cobbler already knew him. He knew him!

6

The Heart of the Matter

"Magowin the cobbler?"

Sam waited about thirty seconds before answering Suzette.

"Magowin the cobbler. Yes. I'm going to meet with Magowin tomorrow to discuss a plan to . . . I suppose, to revive my business and pay for this house and—"

"It's just that—"

"I know, I know. He's a shoemaker. . . . I can't really explain how or why I'm going to see him. But I am. And I think I'm supposed to help him make some shoes while I'm there, which is even stranger!" At this, Sam found a smile creeping over his mouth as he sensed—and somewhat enjoyed—the humor in what he found himself explaining . . . or rather not explaining.

Suzette stammered, "N n no, it's just that I can't believe, or rather . . . I don't know what to say."

"It does sound silly, doesn't it? But I promise, I'll just oblige him this once—"

"No, you don't understand!"

Sam suddenly realized that Suzette's eyes were filled with tears. "What you don't understand is that for two years I have been commissioned on many occasions to sew clothes and coats for the neediest people on the outskirts of the town. And each time, it has been Magowin the cobbler who has commissioned the clothes and paid for every article. Once a month he collects the clothes and takes them with several pairs of shoes to the stone church just past the market. Every month he arrives—whistling and smiling and joyful. And every month I wonder how he affords to pay for so many articles of clothing. I don't charge full price because it's for the needy, but still, it's so much money for Magowin, and. . . . And the other day, after you announced that you would try to get another loan, I found myself in tears beside my bed. And I cried and prayed for hours, Sam. I cried and prayed that we could find a better way to live and work and pay our bills, a way that does not include such misery. And I prayed that God would bless us with the abundance and happiness that I see in Magowin every month. . . . And now you say you're to help him make shoes. . . . Sam, it's the most wonderful news I've heard since you asked me to marry you."

Suzette and Sam embraced for a long time. They had no words.

. . .

So it was that Sam entered the shop of Magowin the cobbler a second time—this time with a lighter step, with the blessing of his wife, and with great hope in his heart.

"Two o'clock! Right on time! Punctuality is a virtue, Sam! So we know we're not starting with an empty slate, eh?" Magowin greeted Sam with a stack of heavy, fragrant leather which he plopped into Sam's arms before directing him to the workbench.

"Well, yes. Right," responded Sam, eager to start the lessons on prosperity.

"Have a seat—I've got some patterns here for you to follow. You've cut leather before, yes?"

"Actually . . . a long time ago in the forest, we—"

"Wonderful! Here are your patterns!" And with that, Sam was immediately set to work on ten pairs of brown leather house shoes while Magowin's own busy activity—cutting, stitching, tanning, servicing customers, drawing up sales—offered the satisfying rhythm and tempo of a happy craftsman at work. By five o'clock, however, after Sam had carved out the last of the soles of the house shoes, he felt compelled to ask Magowin during a quiet lull, "I've learned much in just three short hours about your trade, Magowin. But tell me, when will we begin our first lesson on making a great deal of money?"

"Never."

Sam stopped, confused. "Never?"

"Never. But we can begin our first lesson on achieving prosperity now."

"Oh. Right."

"Right!" echoed Magowin with enthusiasm. "The first thing you need to do is kneel with me now—you can put those tools to the side there. Come, kneel with me here, and together we will give praise to God for the great riches in your life!"

Sam began to realize that he might very well remain in a state of agreeable confusion with Magowin as his teacher. "Praise for what? I can't do that, Magowin. First of all, I'm so in debt and in need of work that I can't possibly praise God for my riches! And . . . and I'm too ashamed to pray to Him right now. Later when I—"

"But, my dear Sam." Magowin's voice became quieter but sternly serious. "I told you I only teach prosperous people. Are you telling me you are not prosperous?"

"Well I've *been* very prosperous. And I will be again, because I'm determined to succeed—I've just got to!" Sam began to feel lost in his words.

"But until you already know how rich you are, I cannot help you, Sam."

"Forgive me, Magowin, but I don't understand. And you simply can't give up on me. My wife, Suzette—she is happier today than I've seen her in years—and I simply can't go back and tell her that you won't teach me."

"Ah, your wife. She means a great deal to you. And your children."

"Oh, Magowin, she is more than I deserve. And my children are a delight . . . but I credit my wife for their rearing. Without Suzette I would surely be a poor man. . . ."

"I see," said Magowin slowly. "And I have compassion for your plight, Sam. But I cannot alter my lesson plan for you. I need to ask you to go back home and not return until you are a prosperous man."

"Magowin, what are you saying?"

"I'm saying, my dear fellow, that you will never reach highest prosperity until you feel worthy of the abundance in your life. And you will not feel worthy until you claim the riches already around you and within you—and dedicate those riches and blessings to the One who gave them to you."

Sam, dumbfounded, walked home slowly, trying to think what to tell Suzette . . . and wondering, Were all those questions he'd answered for himself late into the night, the night before, been in vain?

. . .

Sam returned the next morning to Magowin's shop with great enthusiasm.

"Magowin! I am blessed. You are right—I have so much to be thankful for! I have a beautiful home and a loving wife and fascinating children! I have fine clothes and one of the best carriages in town! I know that I must be thankful for all this in order to work even harder at keeping my abundance. Now can we begin my lessons?"

Magowin looked up with a benevolent, broad smile that stretched from ear to ear. "You have been *thinking,* Sam. I can see that. But you have not been *feeling.* No, Sam, we may not begin—the riches you name are not eternal. Though I *will* say that you will find more joy in the love of your family than in your possessions. If you lost your home and clothes and carriage, would you then feel destitute?"

"Horribly," acknowledged Sam.

"If you were to find yourself alone for a year or more—without your loving wife and children—would you still feel like a man with abundance?"

"Indeed not! How could I?" exclaimed Sam.

"Then you must *experience* and claim that which fills your life with meaning and worth and which endures, no matter what."

Again Sam returned home with a weary mind. The chill in the air reminded him that it was time to stock up on firewood for the coming winter. How would he afford to buy wood this year? His one remaining contract and Suzette's sewing work would not bring in enough money for the mortgage, the food, the expenses, and the firewood. "I'll have to gather my own wood," thought Sam with a sense of shame and defeat.

When he returned home, he greeted Suzette with a warm smile but a heavy heart. Saying very little, he told her quietly that, after briefly checking in on his crewmen, he would spend the rest of the day tending to their winter firewood needs.

He hitched up his horse and drove one of his two work carts to the woods—to the old familiar area of his youth where he had dreamed dreams and where, apparently, he was still the only one who used its wood—and set about gathering locust and oak that only now was beginning to rot. The first half hour was depressing for him, but within the next hour Sam's heart felt less burdened. He began to enjoy the solitude and simplicity of his task at hand, and he gave thanks for the saw he now had, to attack the trees' thicker limbs. After the second hour of work, Sam was astonished to find that he was whistling! Whistling, he thought. What was it that Magowin had told him? Oh, yes: *What you need is to rediscover how to whistle.*

In this quiet forest Sam suddenly felt at peace, free of daily cares and duties. He remembered back to when he had last felt such peace, and with a small laugh he pictured that young Sam who had left his village with great dreams and a feeling of self worth and abundance in his heart. . . . *with a feeling of being worthy of abundance in his life!* . . . He *had* felt that before! How had it come to be? How had it been lost?

Sam searched his mind and tried to think how he could put himself in that place again. He thought so hard, he became frustrated and impatient with himself. Finally his heart called out, "Oh, God!"

The cry reverberated through the trees and bounced back through the sunlight filtering through the whispering leaves.

And his own past methods dawned on Sam.

He knelt down and pressed his hands to his face for quite a while until the words poured out like liquid gold. "Dear God, I used to talk with You every day when I lived in the forest. You were the source of my energy and the source of my comfort. I heard You tell me it was time to leave my home and begin a new path—to use my talents and discover more joy in life. And I did. I really did. . . . But I forgot You somewhere along the way, and now I'm in another kind of forest—a forest of enticements, falsehoods, greed, and self-serving desires. And I need Your guidance, love, and direction to find the happiness I once knew. I see now how blessed I am just to be Your creation. I know how blessed I am to be married to Suzette and to share our beautiful children. I thank You with all my heart and all my soul. My eyes, ears, and heart are open to Your teachings, God, and I accept Your leadership and the great abundance in my life. . . ."

. . .

Sam unloaded his great stacks of firewood, leaving one large pile in his cart. He greeted Suzette with an embrace that said, "I'm home."

. . .

The next day Sam opened Magowin's door, very somberly, very humbly. "Magowin, forgive me, but I must ask you to come with me to deliver some firewood. I have it in my cart and Suzette and I very much wish to give it to a needy family. You will know where it should go."

Magowin put down his work, closed up his shop without a word, and nodded to Sam. They both climbed up onto the wooden seat and Magowin directed Sam to a small house just at the edge of town. "Back here, Sam. We will stack it here."

Quickly and quietly the two men unloaded and stacked the wood next to the house, then left without a word to the woman and children they saw playing inside. On the way back Magowin noted, "You are kind to give this wood, Sam."

"It is not out of kindness, Magowin, but out of thankfulness. You see, God has given me so much that I wanted to thank Him. I used to be a praying man, Magowin. I used to commune with God and He filled my heart with dreams and hope. Then I stopped. . . . I don't know why or how, but I did. And now I want to reclaim the wonder of that relationship. I want to once again feel that it is enough just to be walking with God, living by His rules, doing what I love, and offering a valuable service. I want this so much I ache, Magowin. And my greatest fear is that I won't be able to hold on to that feeling. . . ."

Magowin put his arm around Sam. "Here we are, Sam. Let's go in. I have some stitching for you to do."

"But, Magowin! You said not to come back until I was prosperous!"

"Do you claim God's love and grace?"

"Yes. With all my heart."

"Do you know in your heart that this love and grace will endure forever?"

"I do know this," said Sam, lowering his head.

"Do you know that it is this love and grace that is the true source of your dreams, talents, and wealth?"

"It is. I truly feel this, Magowin."

"You have embraced wisdom, Sam. You have entered the door that leads to fulfillment. You have claimed the wealth of God's wisdom, which will empower you with an honorable life that cannot be measured in gold. It will give you a real hope that radiates from you to everyone you meet. You are now a rich man, Sam."

Sam meekly asked, "But how do I hold on to this feeling and knowing? I am but a man with many faults."

"That's another lesson, Sam. For now, let's celebrate your great wealth by stitching some house shoes!"

7

Stitching a Life Together

And so Sam and Magowin commenced upon the stitching of ten pairs of slip-on house shoes that afternoon. They worked with some whistling, some wincing over pricked fingers, some laughing, some grumbling, and some good-natured comparison of stitching techniques.

"You are a spiritual man, Magowin," reflected Sam at a quiet moment.

"Are we not all spiritual men and women?" said Magowin, closely inspecting one of Sam's house shoes.

"Well, what I mean . . . what I'm wondering . . . is how have you remained so . . . so . . ."

Magowin looked up. "On track?"

Sam laughed. "Yes! I guess that's what I mean."

"I choose it so."

Sam stopped in midstitch. "Choose? But everyone who chooses to live correctly and honorably does not keep in touch with God and goodness."

"No. People may *want* to be honorable, but they don't always make a conscious and heartfelt decision to *choose* to be so. I have chosen to allow Wisdom and Truth to guide my decisions and to frame my decisions within the priority structure that allows for true freedom and lasting success. I follow a set of laws—and the first two are like a set of doors to the path of true prosperity—that is what you are seeking, Sam. These two doors are set in the spiritual realm, but together they lead to success not only in that realm but also here in the material world as well—"

"Wait, wait. You're losing me, Magowin," Sam interrupted. "I want to understand this."

The old cobbler laughed. "Sometimes, Sam, I lose myself!" And then Magowin began the discussion Sam had been craving. "These first two laws, as I said, are like two doors—they are the spiritual laws that one must accept and live by to walk the path to highest fulfillment. The first door is the Law of Wisdom—claiming and believing that the Creator is the source of highest wisdom and truth. The second door is the Law of Priority—the acceptance that your own man-made priority list cannot serve you well. You enter this door—this law—when you accept that your priorities must be heartfelt and inspired by the Divine's plan for your life. This acceptance, of course, doesn't mean your human mind may not rebel at first. . . ." Magowin paused to smile. "And that is why this is actually a spiritual law. The Law of Priority is an act of faith and surrender to the priorities that God reveals to us in almost every facet of life. And these doors can only be entered with a spiritual heart and openness to speaking with God."

"Magowin, please help me understand this Law of Priority." Sam moved the leather shoe parts aside. "Is it not enough that I want . . . that I choose . . . to live a prayerful life in communion with the Creator?"

"Keep stitching, Sam. You will be helping me greatly if we can have those shoes ready by tomorrow."

"Certainly!" exclaimed Sam as he pulled the materials back in front of him. "It's just that I thought the lesson was under way."

"These lessons you must learn with your heart. And your heart must be free to accept the truth within the lesson. And your heart is most free during productive work. That is part of wisdom."

Sam resumed his stitching without a word.

"To answer your question, Sam. . . . You can enjoy a blessed life with God by retreating into the woods and living as a hermit. But tell me. . . . When you were in the forest and you felt the desire to return to grace and clarity of purpose, were you simply resting quietly for hours?"

"Oh, my, no! I was working very hard, gathering and loading wood!"

"Ah—what a blessing work is, yes? You see, Sam, we are working beings, and we find our greatest happiness and worth if we live with God's wisdom in our daily life of work, family, community, and even the drudgery of life."

Sam sighed. "Magowin, this seems easy for you to say, but it was this same daily business you describe and my need to excel at *work* that took my mind *away* from living a simple life."

Magowin looked over at Sam with sincere understanding. "I know, Sam. I know your concern and I know your fear. I know that it is this second door that looms like an impossible entryway to true happiness." The azure eyes looked off into the room as if lost in a memory. "That is why this is also a door requiring faith. It is not enough to experience the spiritual power of God and accept that His wisdom is supreme. If that were enough, we would all be blissfully happy. But God created us in His image, Sam, and that is why we are creative beings with passions, drives, desires, the need to work and produce—and the need to love." Magowin paused, then turned to Sam. "So you know where we go wrong? We associate that human part of life with the physical only! We don't take our spiritual commitment into our daily life. Do you really think it was work and duty and family and "life" that kept you away from God? Or could it be that it did not occur to you to take God and His wisdom with you to work and into your home and while you washed dishes and while you negotiated a contract?"

Sam, of course, knew the answer.

"Priority, Sam," Magowin continued. "Very important. Without it we are locked out of highest prosperity. We can have a beautiful spiritual connection to God as we walk in the woods, but if that is the only place we talk to God, then we'll not live fully—our lives will not be truly significant."

Sam was aghast. "I want my life to be significant!"

"Good. Commit your heart—commit your life—to living by the Divine's priorities. The Creator will not lead you astray —but it's not enough to *intellectually* proclaim that this is how to live." Magowin tapped Sam on the forehead, then laid his hand on Sam's chest. "You must feel it with faith. You must feel that God loves you enough to direct you in your work—and His work. The work you've agreed to do together. He really needs you, Sam, and you really need Him."

Sam was inspired and feeling hopeful. "How do I know these priorities?"

"The first is clear. Love and honor and listen to God's wisdom. Keep the Law of Wisdom as your foundation. Pray for guidance with faith that you will be led. Live knowing that God is beside you and will place you in circumstances that enable you to get on track—if you listen with your heart and maintain a dialog with God."

"I'm still not sure. . . . I *know* you are right, but . . ."

"You must *feel* that I'm right, Sam. You must feel to your core that if you do not prioritize what you think about, what you attend to, what you pray for, what you finish, what you say, and what you value—that your life will be utterly miserable! God is not just an ethereal wispy feeling of oneness with the universe." Magowin swept his hand through the air with a dramatic flourish. "He's a vigorous part of our daily experiences. He's involved with what we choose to create in life—and when He creates with us, we produce more than our dreams can imagine. Makes you want to regroup and prioritize, doesn't it, Sam?"

Sam nodded—vigorously.

"Wonderful! Go home and share your heart with Suzette about what you feel and what we've talked about. Then, together—very important, Sam—together, prioritize everything you can think of—from how you spend your time, to what warrants disciplinary action with your children—assuming that they misbehave at times—"

"Oh, yes," sighed Sam.

"—to what your expenditures should be, and where your energies should be placed."

"Will that tell us what God's priorities are?"

"It's a start. It will tell you that you can't do it on your own—that you need God's help. That I can assure you."

"We will discuss all this at my next lesson? And what about all those questions you asked me to think about when I first met you?"

"Ah! You see . . . you have asked the right question at precisely the right time! Do you see why I thoroughly enjoy that the Creator helps me with my teaching work?" Magowin's face broke out into the gleeful smile of a child. "You and Suzette are to discuss those questions—you'll know why as you talk! They will reveal where you've come from, so you'll know what you must change in order to reprioritize and get where you're going."

"And our next lesson?"

"You will learn the next law . . . but I won't be your teacher."

"What? What do you mean? Who will I go to see?"

"She'll teach you when your ears are open and you will know the truth of her words. She is an expert on this third law, and you will be wise to heed her authority."

"Who . . . where . . . ?" Sam was searching for information he must have missed.

"So! Start tonight! This is not an easy assignment. Most people fail here—don't you fail, Sam!"

"Yes. Of course." Sam fumbled with the leather pieces still in front of him and began to stack them neatly in order to go home.

"Uh—but we must finish stitching these shoes! I will have customers tomorrow who will need comfortable house shoes for wearing while they cook dinner, read to their children, clean their chimneys, wash clothes . . . or attend to a sick wife. . . . Very important that we finish! And then you may go home to plan your life."

And so he did.

8

The Fire Talk

The children were put to bed, the dishes were cleared and washed, the curtains drawn, and the fire stoked. Sam and Suzette sat before the hearth quietly, holding hands, waiting for the other to begin.

"I think . . ." began Sam.

"We can . . ." began Suzette.

The two laughed softly.

"You think what, Sam?"

"We can what, Suzette?" They laughed a bit more as the room warmed.

"I think we should pray."

"We can begin with prayer."

They looked at each other and smiled, knowing that their lives were about to change.

Silently they prayed, each with a heart open to God's compassion, love, and strength. Silently they prayed, each feeling peace at that moment. Silently they prayed that God would lead their way. He had always wanted to lead them—toward true fulfillment, trust, and openness to life and love. Then, together, they prayed aloud, each giving thanks to the Creator who held them in His arms, each asking for guidance and grace, each acknowledging that life can only be lived fully by living within His divine plan. Amen.

Sam and Suzette looked into each other's eyes—a bit self-consciously but full of hope for their future. Then they began the difficult discussion that faced them—somehow, they were over their heads financially, and worse, negativity and frustration had eaten away at the fabric of their home and marriage. Sam dejectedly offered that he was the cause of all their problems. Suzette assured him that they were in this together. Back and forth they went until Suzette firmly countered, "Let's stop, stop recounting the errors. Stop blaming and punishing yourself, stop making me the long-suffering wife, stop searching for the way out."

Sam blinked. "But we must find a way out. And with God's help—"

"We *are* out, Sam. With God's help we *are* out. Just because we need to honor our financial commitments and change our outlooks doesn't mean we're still stuck where we were, don't you see? We're out. We're *here.* From here we start. Thank God we're here at this moment with new resolve and new hearts. We have so much already, Sam. . . ."

Sam hugged Suzette. "My dear love. You are beautiful. You are precious. And you are right. How could I forget Magowin's first lesson—that no one will live a rich life until he knows that he is rich already. We *do* have much, Suzette, and today we begin a new path."

"It won't be easy."

"No, it won't be easy," admitted Sam. "But it will be right."

"So, we begin now, yes? We begin not by listing our debts but by listing our joys, blessings, and worth."

"Listing! Yes! When I first met with Magowin, he sent me home to think about—Oh, Suzette, he asked me to think about so many questions, they whirled in my head. I don't know if I can remember them all, but he asked me today to go over them with you during this . . . this discussion."

Suzette smiled. She knew how Sam disliked "discussions." And she knew how she loved this man, despite watching him slide into misery in the last few years. Through it all she had remained true to her small sewing business and teaching the children their lessons. Through it all she had kept her heart and mind on her work, as a businesswoman and as a wife, mother, and community member. And though this had sustained her, she'd known that the day would come when Sam's pride and foundationless world would crumble. But she had also known that there was a strong foundation they would rediscover—together—to rebuild upon.

Still smiling, Suzette asked, "And those questions?"

"If I can remember. . . . And we're to go over them so that we can begin to prioritize."

"Of course. That's fine. The first question?"

"Well, Magowin asked me 'Who are you really, Sam, and why do you want to be prosperous?'"

Suzette laughed. "Surely this is not the very first question!"

"No . . . but he did ask the impossible. He asked that I review my entire life. And think about how I was raised to view wealth and money. How my family made a living, and what they and the villagers taught me. What my beliefs about saving and giving and spending were. I was also to think about what I enjoyed about my work, what I think about at work. It's so much, Suzette—but I stayed up all night that night trying to think about what I think about! Oh, and, uh . . . he asked me how much I include you in my financial decisions, and why I was attracted to you. . . ."

"Oh, I like that one! Do you know why I was attracted to you?" Suzette glanced sideways at Sam.

"I believe I charmed you." Sam returned her glance.

"My dear husband: I fell in love because I saw a noble, searching soul in you. I saw a man who loved his work and was kind to his fellow workers. I saw a man who stopped to help strangers and who took the time to study the craftsmanship of more experienced tradesmen. And I saw a man who looked at me with true love in his eyes—and so I suppose you did charm me . . . a bit. But I'm more pragmatic than that, Sam. I saw God working through your heart, and this was by far the quality that drew me to you. I felt that God had brought you into my life—and I still feel that way."

Sam looked down. "Suzette, I don't know what to say. Surely I have disappointed you."

"Do you love God? Do you love me and the children?"

"Of course. With all my heart."

"Then I can never be disappointed. . . . You haven't told me how you answered that question. What attracted you to me?"

"My love! I was attracted to you because I thought . . . I still think . . . that you are incredibly special. You are wise, patient, talented, and radiant. I could think of no greater blessing in my life than to have such a special woman share her life with me. You are simply beautiful. I love you so much, Suzette. I want to share everything with you."

"Even your financial decisions? Even your money and borrowing decisions?"

Sam looked down again. "I think that part is difficult. . . . I think . . ."

"Don't think. Talk. Start. Here we go. Let's start discussing our financial backgrounds and all the questions Magowin suggested. I'll start."

It was a long discussion. A long discussion between a man raised as a wood gatherer in rather poor conditions during his dreamy youth, and a woman raised much more comfortably as the daughter of shepherds who lived in a small hut on the grounds of a large manor house. A long discussion between a man who never learned to read, but who could calculate sums and figures and devise new tools, and a woman who was tutored in the manor house by the gracious mistress. A long discussion between two people who loved each other dearly and shared much in common.

It lasted well into the evening. Sam arose several times to add wood to the fire—especially when the "discussion" hinted at becoming heated. Sam wanted all the finest things for the children. Suzette wanted their children to lead fine lives. Sam was very nervous about possibly giving up their large home. Suzette did not care what any townsfolk might think. They discussed the children's lessons, what they should teach them about money, life, and spiritual matters. They discussed each other's spending habits, their saving habits—or nonsaving habits—and who should be included in a variety of financial decisions—a difficult subject for anyone with a human nature!

But discuss they did, and they indeed kept coming back to their main focus—loving and listening to God to guide them through all matters.

"This is our first priority, Suzette. I know it, though I feel myself so afraid to simply follow what my heart tells me—even though I recapture that amazing certainty during prayer and reflection, like the other day in the forest. Yes, this is the first priority. And from here we are to prioritize all else. This is what Magowin said. And I know it to be true."

They took a long quiet moment staring at the fire. They each took a deep breath, then they began the subject of priorities. The spiritual needs of the family and the children. The spiritual needs of each other. Which forms of misbehavior from the children warranted what degree of discipline. The priority of love and praise over pointing out faults. How to respond to mishaps and crises, and finally, how to respond to the most pressing crisis in Sam's mind—the mortgage, the bills, the financial pressures.

"I feel that earning enough to pay the bills should be a high priority—this will serve my family and myself."

"If you earn enough, that is wonderful, Sam. But if you do not, will you feel like a failure? Surely your priority should be to work diligently so as to earn an honest income—and with that income we will see what we can afford."

"But the house—"

"The house can be sold or turned over to Geoffrey the moneylender."

"Oh, no . . . I can't—"

"Remember your priorities, Sam. The house will not make us happy if you are miserably focused on earning more and more and more. Tell me, Sam, what *is* your goal in life?" Suzette playfully nudged Sam.

Sam relaxed and asked with some amusement, "You mean, 'Who are you really, Sam, and why do you want to be prosperous?'"

Suzette laughed. "I guess so."

"I truly want to be successful in a building business. I want it so much. I love the feel of wood and stone in my hands. I love designing and crafting a new home or building, and the camaraderie of a fine crew. I have lost my zeal . . . my crew is not too pleased to be working with me, and I find that very painful in my heart. Who am I? I'm a rather simple wood gatherer, I suppose, who dreamed of creating something better for myself and the people I love. I'm a man who now faces uncertainty. For, tomorrow I begin the last contract on my books. Tomorrow I begin while knowing that I have not succeeded in earning a living at what I love to do—or at least what I once loved to do. . . ."

"Sam. . . . Please don't—"

"Suzette, we *did* need this discussion, and I know I must trust God and I must confer with you more concerning my . . . well, my rather rash financial and personal decisions. But this does not tell me what I am to do about the next mortgage payment—which is due in three weeks time."

"In three weeks your project will be completed—or nearly completed," offered Suzette. "Concentrate on your building. When the due date arrives, then we'll concern ourselves with the house payment. For now, just love your work—truly love it—feel blessed by it and love those who work for you."

"Suzette, you make this sound so simple."

"It's you who have made your motive too complicated. Your motive is money and prestige and more, more, more. So, indeed, I'm sure my words do sound oversimplified."

The words stung, and Sam was silent.

"Sam, I know all is not so simple." She was quiet for a long time. Then she asked, "Why do we discipline and teach the children?"

Sam looked blankly at Suzette. "Because we are their parents."

"I believe the answer is more simple than that. If we did it just because we're their parents, that would mean it was merely a duty—and a duty can only motivate for so long. Duty is not our core motive in helping to steer them. Answer again, Sam. Why do we put so much effort into showing them the way? There is a much simpler answer."

Sam stared into the fire, then looked at his patient wife. "Because we want to. Because we love them."

"We love them," echoed Suzette. "That's our true motivating force. Our love for life and God and this earth flows into our love for them. Not just because they are our blood and in our care, but because they are children—ours and God's—and we can't help but love them unconditionally. We so naturally act on that love that we don't even think about love as our motive."

"You're right. Of course that's right. You're right that we are not motivated by duty but by abiding love. But what has this to do with my work?"

Suzette kissed Sam's cheek. "I believe it has everything to do . . . with everything!"

Sam looked at Suzette. Her eyes were dancing, radiant with joy, alive with hope and a childlike certainty. "Suzette," he marveled, "you're aglow. What do you have that makes you sparkle like that?"

"Do you know why I work, Sam? Do you know why I look forward to my sewing commissions?"

"Well, because you love sewing and crafting fine clothing and linens, and because you do it so well and are rewarded for your work."

"That is only part. Yes, it's what I do well, and I'm naturally gifted with these talents. I know they're God-given talents, and my God has asked me to use them. He has also asked me to love, so I use my work to love others."

Sam listened, knowing that his wife was revealing quiet but profound wisdom to him.

"Sam, I truly love my customers—even the grouchy ones! When I sew a buttonhole, I imagine that man or woman preparing for the day, and I love that person. So I put love into that buttonhole. When I stitch a flower onto a baby coverlet, I love that new child yet to be born. So I entwine love into that stitching. Do my customers know? I'm not always sure. But I'm not motivated by whether or not they know that I love them—or that I send my love through my work to them. Somehow, though, I believe it does show through and God blesses me for loving others. I have never been wanting for customers or work. This love for others is what inspires and motivates me to work. It enables me to serve through my skill, and I am blessed with monetary payment in return."

Silence again, except for the crackling fire. . . .

"And I know, dear wife, that you are going to tell me how this relates to me."

"I have the most intelligent husband!" Suzette kissed Sam's cheek again. "Sam, you must not simply love your work—your physical labor or what you create—and you most certainly must not love the monetary rewards of work. That is misplaced love—and motive. If money is your motive, you will fail at finding happiness, I assure you. You must love God and His wisdom, you must set your priorities according to His wisdom, you must love other people and you must find a way to serve them that utilizes your talents. Your motive must be love—real, unconditional love."

"You're saying I need to love the people who have asked me to build this house?"

"Yes. It's that simple. You must forget money and concentrate on loving your customers and those who will live in the house. You must love your workers and you must love what you and God are creating together."

"Hmm. These folks are not particularly popular—somewhat surly, I'm afraid. I'm the only one from three towns around who agreed to take on their project. They can be mean-spirited, and I know they'll complain at every step."

"You must love them. God doesn't ask us to love just the

sweet people, or those whom we feel to be in need of love. *All* are in need. Find it, Sam. Find within yourself a desire to let yourself be motivated by love. It's there. I know you too well. You're afraid to let this motivate you because you fear it will interfere with profits."

The truth always rings with a pure tone. And Sam knew he had heard wisdom and truth in those words. "This . . . I must think on . . ." he said slowly.

"It's time to sleep. We're both weary from this important discussion. I love you, Sam. And, bless you, in a few short hours you will rise to start the house of those cranky customers who need your love!" They both laughed, and tension and worry dissolved.

Thus they ended the late, late evening with some humored and hopeful hearts. . . .

And the next day . . .

. . . Sam kissed Suzette goodbye and went off to begin a new job with a new heart. He met his crew at dawn at the cleared sight. They stood beside the stacks of lumber and stone and awaited Sam's first "commands."

But instead Sam stood there, just looking at the men, then looking at his shoes, then off in the distance. Finally words came.

"My fellow workers. Today we begin not a building but a home. Today you are not a laborer but a dream maker. Today you have the opportunity to begin a work you will be proud of—a work that will bring joy to those who will live in this home."

The men were stunned. Who was this man before them? What had happened to the usual barking of orders that set them in motion? How were they supposed to respond to this approach?

Sam went on. "Men, today we add something to our building materials that I have been leaving out for far too long. Today we add something more permanent than mortar, more enduring than stone, more rich than fine wood. Today we add love."

Naturally, the men were still silent—in fact they had become uncomfortable and irritated. Had Sam lost his wits because he was no longer successful? Had he gone silly?

"Thomas!"

The crew snapped to attention.

"Thomas, you will lead the crew today in forming and laying the stones for the foundation. All stones are to be set meticulously, taking great care to maintain the level. And, Thomas, we will not use the inferior timber for the flooring as we have done in the past. We will use the finest, strongest wood. And do you know why?"

"Um . . . because the master and mistress have asked for this?"

"No, Thomas. It is because we should. Because if we truly love these people and the grandchildren who will someday play upon these floors, then we will want these floors to be sturdy and pleasant to walk upon. We want these owners to have peace of mind that these floors will wear well and resist rotting. We want these floors to reflect that we care—not just about our project but about these people. As we construct the stone foundation we will think on this—that this foundation will support a fine floor. Let us begin."

And so they did. And as they constructed the foundation on the neatly graded dirt, the men whispered and confided among themselves that surely Sam was not quite himself. And yet, they did not disapprove of his guidance and motivational words. Indeed, these men all took great pride in their work and welcomed this new tone. By the middle of the day, someone had started whistling. By the end of the day a sturdy, well-crafted, and level foundation was ready.

"Thank you, men. Together we have done a good job. I am blessed to have you on this crew. We meet again tomorrow morning."

That evening Sam recounted the day to Suzette. "I am applying your words of wisdom. I think the men find it a bit amusing, but I intend to stress that this is our labor of love until the end. And at the end . . ."

"At the end, Sam, we will see what money we have and visit the moneylender. That's all there is to discuss on that matter, yes? For now, enjoy this soup and bread I've prepared." Then Suzette added with a twinkle in her eye, "For I have prepared it with love because I knew you would be eating it!"

. . .

True to his intent, Sam directed the crew at every step to think about the people who would enjoy their new house. When the owners inspected, they sometimes found fault in ways that sorely tested Sam's resolve. But Sam insisted to his crew that they were not to think on the unhappiness shown by these folks, but rather the happiness that perhaps the house might offer them.

The more he expressed this motivation, the more he felt it come truly alive within him. The more he talked of the importance of each detail, the more he felt at peace with the work. The more he concentrated on the giving aspect of his work, the more joy and fulfillment he got from his work. . . . And so did his men.

Every window was crafted with love for anyone who would open its shutters and greet the day. The hearth was carefully designed and constructed to exude warmth—even without a fire! The doors were smoothly sanded to be lovely to the touch. Ledges were added to walls to hold flower vases and family mementos. The roof was pitched more steeply than Sam had recently designed. This was difficult for Sam and the roofers, but Sam knew that only the steep roofs in the village withstood the rains, the sleeting, and the snow that caused "usual fare" roofs to leak, crack, or even cave in.

Each evening Sam told Suzette of the progress, and each evening Suzette welcomed home a man who had a lighter step and a lighter heart—a man who loved his work and had found a way to love his customers.

The house was nearly completed and the mortgage due

date was approaching. Sam knew he would need to set an appointment with Geoffrey the moneylender. And so he went after work on a Friday.

When Geoffrey answered his door, Sam very calmly asked if he could set a time to discuss his loan—next week when he would bring by the mortgage payment.

"That would be suitable. Next Friday—anytime after the midday meal, I'll be here."

"Next Friday, yes. The afternoon it is. And I will be bringing my wife, Suzette."

"Certainly," responded Geoffrey in his unusually soft voice. "I think that is most wise."

"Thank you, good man. I will return in a week." Sam was amazed at how relaxed he felt. He was buoyed by the success he felt with this house, and he had not thought about the profit from it—or rather, he had not been distracted with thoughts of the profit. He was feeling so calm that, when he passed Magowin's little cobbler shop, he paused—and then went in, of course!

"Sam!" Magowin's face broke into a wide, jubilant grin as he came forward to usher his student and friend into his shop.

"I see you are making black leather boots, Magowin. Very fancy."

"Ho-ho, my friend! They are for the duchess and her daughters. They are avid horsewomen, you know. You look well, my young student!"

"Ah, Magowin, you warm my heart. I miss you. But I have been very, very busy with a house. . . ."

"I know of this new house. It is four streets over. There is good talk of this house. Very good talk. It is said that the crew is in love with this house and that everyone is envious of the future owners. They are getting more than they bargained for, eh?" Magowin's eyes were twinkling.

Sam laughed. "I suppose you're right. But this house has helped me come out of a mournful state, so I do not regret a small loss of profit. This house has been a blessing, for I know

now what is truly most enjoyable about my labor. To be of service and to work with love and an honorable spirit."

"Your wheels have certainly been set in motion," marveled Magowin. "I fear I have no hope of your giving up on the building trade to join me in the footwear business!"

"Ha! One never knows," laughed Sam. "I have no prospects as yet. But I'm more motivated now than I've felt in years. I'm very hopeful that I can help with another project soon."

"And what motivates you, Sam?" Magowin eyed him keenly.

"This may sound rather simple . . . but love motivates me. I want to love people the way I used to. I want to offer them my service and my talents, and I want to work knowing that I have contributed to their lives in some way. I want to see my business not just as a source of income, but as a way for me to express my love for life and for others."

"You want to build with God at your side."

"Yes, Magowin. I have not forgotten the Laws of Wisdom and Priority. They have led me to this new outlook. Actually, Suzette, my wise and persistent wife reminded me of what my focus should be. She is an amazing woman, Magowin."

"Yes, and an amazing teacher! Did I not say that your next teacher would be an expert on the third law?"

"The third law? What do you mean? Suzette? How . . . ?"

"The third law is the Law of Motive. Until you acknowledge with your heart and soul that the highest motive in all actions and all work is to love others and to seek to serve them, you can never achieve true, lasting prosperity."

Sam was in awe of what flooded through him. "How did you know she would lead me to this?" whispered Sam.

"Because I know her work. And I see love in it. I see love in her eyes as she hands me the clothes that I purchase to give to the poor. Never once—never, Sam—has she skimped on those clothes, even though she does not charge me full price for them. Every article is stitched to withstand a hundred washings. The embroidery is flawless. You should see the mothers who receive Suzette's dresses and bed linens and curtains. Their eyes are filled with gratitude; the women are overwhelmed by the obvious love that has gone into each piece. And you ask how I knew that Suzette would teach you about the blessing of putting love into work?" Magowin slapped Sam on the back. "My very wonderful man, how could I *not* know? All that was needed was for your heart and ears to be open!"

"And . . . does this mean that I'm to learn the fourth law soon? Am I to rejoin you in your shop after all?"

"No fears, Sam! You will be building again soon, I have faith in this. No, you must visit Geoffrey to learn the fourth law."

"Geoffrey! How strange that you should say this! I have an appointment with him in one week . . . regarding my debt!"

"Hmm . . . regarding your debt. Well, yes, he'll undertake that matter with you, of course, but he will teach you something, also, about freedom."

"Freedom? Magowin, you puzzle me, but I have learned to trust your every word."

Magowin smiled very warmly into Sam's trusting eyes. "I am so happy to hear this, Sam, because I craft my words with love, knowing that they will fall not only upon your ears but into your heart."

9

Payment Plans

Sam and his loyal crew had attracted attention during the building of the home "built with love." Every day, townspeople had strolled by to watch the progress and listen to the cheery camaraderie of the men who seemed to take such pride in this one small house.

And they had asked questions. Why was the path to the door not straight, but elegantly curved? "Because there is to be a planting of flowers beneath this tree and we thought it would be nice for the owners to walk past that spot as they come home each day."

Why was there a ramp built up to the back stoop? "So that water buckets can be brought into the house by cart. Won't that be more convenient for the owners?"

The townspeople marveled that the crew cared about the comfort of the owners. Their craftsmanship was superb. And the singing and whistling in jovial harmony was uplifting. To be sure, a stop to see "the house" had become a must every day—even for the busiest tradesmen and for harried mothers with children in tow.

. . .

The day before his scheduled meeting with Geoffrey, Sam received the third of four installment payments on the project. The tax collector showed up at the site to collect the King's share—taking time to admire this cozy home that seemed to have its own warm spirit.

The tax collector felt uncomfortable hanging about—he was not a well-received figure—but this home looked so inviting. It was just the kind he would love to have for his wife and new baby boy. Catching Sam's attention and pulling him aside, he hesitantly asked Sam when he would be available to build a home for his family.

"My good man," replied Sam, "I am not as busy as you might suppose. I can begin in about one week's time—when this home is finished."

"So soon!" The tax collector's heart was joyous. "Truly? I will draw up the papers! My wife will be very happy. I have not dared to ask anyone to build a house for me. . . . I feared no one would, or that they might try to cheat me somehow. I am not well liked. I have my job, you see, and . . . I am not well liked."

Sam clapped the tax collector on the back. "My team would be honored to create a home for your family. And we will give you only our best work!" Then with a chuckle he added, "What better way to again see some of those coins that I have handed over to you today, yes?"

. . .

That evening, Sam and Suzette readied for their meeting with the loan agent. The mortgage payment was eight hundred royal coins and, after Sam's crew had been paid their share, they still had twelve hundred. They were relieved that they held enough for tomorrow—but sad not to have enough to cover both the next month's expenses and the following mortgage payment. With no firm contracts in hand, Sam released himself to admitting that they should probably not keep their house. Yet, somehow, this did not upset him as it would have just a month earlier.

The next day at noon, Sam and Suzette cheerfully took the children to the neighbor's and went on to Geoffrey's with quiet resolve.

"Come in, please. I've prepared us some tea." Geoffrey

ushered them in and greeted them in his usual hushed tone. One had to listen intently to catch all Geoffrey's words. They were few and always spoken softly.

Once seated, Sam spoke up. "Geoffrey, I'll get right to the point. We've brought the payment, but I cannot guarantee that we will have next month's payment. I have eight hundred coins for you"—Sam placed a strong cloth pouch before Geoffrey—"and I have four hundred still in my purse. I will receive one more payment in a week, when my project is complete, which will indeed give me eight hundred coins, but as you know, there will be food to buy and expenses for this coming month. Suzette will have earnings from her business, and I do have someone interested in having a house built, but at this time I have no contract in hand." Sam took a breath. "So, I am in need of your . . . well, your advice as to how to proceed. Should we pay extra interest and put off paying for a few months until I'm back on my feet? Should we sell the house or turn it over? We're at a loss as to how to handle this obligation." Sam looked at his hands, then at Suzette, then back to Geoffrey.

Geoffrey looked gently at the two before him. "And so . . ." he began. Sam and Suzette leaned forward to hear him clearly. "So you will have at least six hundred forty coins for the upcoming month. Will this get you through?" He looked at Suzette.

"Six hundred forty? Well, that would not be enough to live on, I'm afraid, but actually we'll have eight hundred from Sam's pay and—"

Geoffrey put up his hand slowly and looked back at Sam. "You will have next month's mortgage, Sam. Take comfort in that. But perhaps you are correct. I think this house of yours is too much for your means . . . and needs."

Sam and Suzette were somewhat confused. Had they heard Geoffrey clearly? What was this 640 figure he was using? And how could he know that Sam would have next month's mortgage?

Sam spoke. "I have foolishly obligated myself to a house

that is too costly and I am ashamed to have borrowed what I cannot easily repay. But what did you just say about . . . ?"

"Marcus the tax collector came in last evening to see me about a loan. For a house. That you will build him. You will build a fine home for this man. You will be blessed to serve him. And I . . . I will have the opportunity to serve him in ways he does not yet realize." Geoffrey's voice was so quiet that Sam and Suzette almost felt as if they were listening to a prayer.

"Yes, you will have next month's mortgage, Sam and Suzette. But this is not my main concern." Again he looked at Suzette. "Six hundred forty coins will not see you through?"

Suzette puzzled over how to respond. "I will have enough. As we said, Sam will have a total of eight hundred coins by next week and I will earn four hundred fifty coins from my sewing. Of course, fifty will go to taxes, but this leaves twelve hundred for the monthly expenses, and this will be sufficient. But why do you want to know about my expenses?"

"My dear Suzette. I care greatly about your financial health. I have no wish for any loan you may have with me to disrupt your happiness or harmony. I wish for you only highest prosperity. Tell me, can you get by on a thousand for the month?"

"A thousand? That would be difficult, but we'll have twelve hundred, Geoffrey—"

Again Geoffrey put up his hand. He smiled warmly at the two. "You have described earnings of two thousand royal coins to me, yes? Twelve hundred so far on Sam's project, four hundred more to come, and Suzette's four hundred."

"Yes, that's right," replied Sam. "We've paid the taxes already, and we're paying eight hundred to you. So that leaves us twelve hundred for the month."

"But have you paid God?"

Sam and Suzette were silent, taken aback. Hesitantly, Suzette said, "We are not selfish people, Geoffrey. Truly not. Each month I sell articles at reduced prices for the poor. It is a joy to do so. And we give money to the church when we can."

"That's fine. That is indeed fine. And I am not here to judge you. It is because I love you and I know that you are seeking God's ways that I bring this up to you. Listen with your heart. Until you give away at least ten percent of your earnings to God's service and those in need, you will not fully appreciate and enjoy your own wealth. Ten percent of these two thousand coins is two hundred. That is your tithe amount."

Sam, whose heart had opened so much in the past months since his meeting with Magowin, suddenly felt cornered and overwhelmed again.

"Geoffrey, you are obviously a man speaking of what is right. And I admit that I have come to you with great anticipation today, for Magowin the cobbler said that you would speak to me of freedom. But right now I only feel more burdened. We are not ready to set aside an additional ten percent of our earnings for the needy. I have committed myself to serving God. We have committed ourselves." Sam took Suzette's hand. "We have opened our minds to His wisdom and guidance. I have discovered a new feeling of peace and joy in serving others through my work. At this time, is this not enough? Must I also give precious coins that my family needs?"

"You do indeed have generous spirits." Geoffrey placed his hands on their clasped hands. "You are blessed. I see this in the house you are building, Sam. I see this in the dresses my wife purchases from you, Suzette. You are walking a true path. But if you are seeking complete freedom—including financial freedom—you must release yourself to giving in all ways, with all your sources of energy. This includes your money."

Geoffrey leaned back and then poured more tea. "Tell me, Sam. If you were a very wealthy man, would you enjoy giving your money for tithes and helping others?"

Sam's face brightened. "Oh, yes! Very much!"

"I see your eyes light up—that would be . . . well, fun, wouldn't it?"

"It would be wonderful to be so generous and benevolent. This would be a dream of mine."

"Then why are you denying yourself this dream?"

Sam was speechless. Geoffrey continued. "Suzette, do Sam's eyes light up like this when he has his horse carts serviced?"

Suzette was relieved to laugh. "No, I should say not!"

"Yet he chooses to own two carts, but gets no pleasure in the financial burden of their upkeep." Geoffrey turned back to Sam. "Does the extra cart give you as much joy as the joy you felt when you thought about benevolent giving?"

"I . . . well I suppose not, but . . ."

"Yes?"

"I'm not a wealthy man yet." Suddenly Sam heard his words and took in a breath. "No. This is not true. I *am* a wealthy man. I am following the laws that Magowin has revealed to me, and the first step was to see myself as blessed and prosperous as a creation of God. I *am* wealthy in many ways, Geoffrey. But not with money . . . at this point."

"But you are on the path to prosperity?"

"Oh, yes!"

"You wish to succeed and prosper in life? You wish to lead a significant life?"

"With all my heart."

"Then you must experience an even deeper partnership with God, by giving back a portion of what you earn to others, whom your Creator also loves and cares for."

"But, Geoffrey, I don't know that I can afford to make my required payments—to you—if I must also give ten percent away."

"Sam, if you cannot afford to give, then you are indeed living beyond your means. You are depriving yourself of great happiness."

Again Sam was silent. Suzette turned to him. "He's right, Sam. We are not getting great joy from our possessions. Some we truly do need, but most are simply things we want—and the pleasure from owning them wears off quickly. I am actually feeling a peace about this. I would rather live more modestly and share our prosperity than live in dread of our bills. We can do this, Sam."

Sam looked off into a corner of the room. "This is not what I expected today. I came to discuss my debt, and I learn that I am to keep even less of my money." Then he turned back to the two who sat before him with true understanding and care in their eyes. "But I will do this, because I know you are telling me truth."

Geoffrey nodded. "And you know that I am not using my influence as your loan agent. Rather, as a person, as a fellow man, I saw this as an opportunity to speak to your heart. You will reach your dreams, Sam, by following this rule to give ten percent—to share your wealth."

"This is the fourth law, isn't it?" Sam looked resolutely into Geoffrey's eyes.

Geoffrey smiled. "The Law of Generosity. It is not merely a duty or a commandment. It is a means to increase your happiness and even your own wealth. It is a law that asks you to accept even more that you are an instrument and partner of God. As you help others, you help those whom God also cherishes. He needs you, Sam and Suzette. He needs your prayers, your devotion, your joys, and your tithes. We will discuss your house payment again next month. Today, take two hundred coins from the four hundred you now hold and take them to the pastor."

Although Sam wondered how they would make it until their next income payment, he agreed to do so.

"Trust God's ways, Sam. Today you will feel great satisfaction and more freedom. Don't analyze this. Have faith in your heart's dream to be a giver. Then come back in a month and tell me not about your debts but about your freedom!"

With very few words, Sam and Suzette thanked Geoffrey, counted out two hundred coins from their purse, secured them in a little pouch, and then proceeded to the small chapel down the road. They looked at each other, withdrew the pouch, and knocked on the wooden door of the pastor's home.

The pastor was a young, enthusiastic man who had only lived in the town a few short years. Already, however, he was beloved. He worked tirelessly to minister to all the people of the town, even those who refused to attend services. As he opened his door, he greeted Sam and Suzette joyfully. "What a blessed surprise! Suzette, I was just mentioning your name! I am hoping to start a school for the children in town. So few can read, you know, and it has always been my dream to share the sacred literature with as many as possible. If I could start a school in my home . . . Oh, what a great blessing this would be to the children—and all adults who wish to learn. And I know, Suzette, that you read and that you teach your own children. I was just mentioning your name in prayer. . . ." Pastor Wright's eyes twinkled as he glanced at Suzette.

Suzette nodded and laughed. "If you need my help, Pastor Wright, I will certainly help in this. I would be honored. Even my oldest child can help instruct the youngest students."

"Praise to God!" exclaimed the young pastor. And with a comical look toward the sky he added, "And now, Father, if you could arrange for the schoolbooks to knock upon my door, I will be even more grateful and truly amazed!"

"Perhaps you can buy them with this." Sam produced the small pouch. "It is but two hundred royal coins, but . . ."

The pastor was stunned. Then the normally exuberant man silently, silently looked at the pouch with tears running down his face. He could not speak.

"Surely they will get the school started," suggested Suzette to break the awkward silence.

Pastor Wright looked up and smiled broadly. "It will, indeed. I thank you. And God thanks you. Your generosity has been perfectly timed."

"You are more than welcome," said Suzette. "I will call on you tomorrow to help plan your school." . . .

And the next day . . .

. . . Suzette was preparing the meal when Sam came through the door. "Where have you been this fine Saturday afternoon with no word to your wife?" she chided him good-naturedly.

"I sold one of my horse carts to Thomas. He's been saving for a long time, and I knew my used one would be less expensive than a new one for him." Sam placed a bag of coins on the table. "Three hundred royal coins. Two hundred are for your household expenses. The other hundred take with you to Pastor Wright's on Monday."

"Sam! You always said that only poor men had but one cart. You will not miss this cart?" Suzette was beaming with pride at her husband.

"I will never miss that cart. And now there are two things that I will possess forever."

Suzette hugged her husband, kissed him, and asked, "And what are they?"

"For as long as I live, I will always have the memory of Thomas's overjoyed face when I offered him such a bargain on my fine cart. And I will always treasure the look on Pastor Wright's face when we handed him those coins in complete faith. Those moments will bring me more joy than that horse cart ever could. Life is becoming exciting, Suzette! I'm famished! What's for supper?"

10

Reality Check

Sam and his crew stood awhile to admire their work. The house was not particularly large, but it was solidly built and seemed to actually say, "Welcome." The stonework was precise, the timber framing was attractive as well as functional, the window ledges were generous (enough for two pies or several flower pots), and even the modest patch of earth that led to the doorway was thoughtfully prepared, complete with paving, some rock terracing, and flowering plants beneath a small oak in front of the house.

This was work to be proud of. This was a place that the new owners could be proud of. And this was a home that would last for several generations—and each generation would know, just by its details and quality construction, that this was a house built with gifted hands and caring hearts.

Sam's own heart was swelling that day. Not only had his crew finished a very successful project together, but he had already received news from Grecco that several more folks had inquired into hiring Sam's crew to build a stable, a shop, another home, and repair several bridges in the area. The slight chill in the air was barely noticeable as Sam glowed with contentment. Silently he praised the Divine for this beautiful day and for leading him on a new path. God bless Suzette for believing in him. God bless Magowin for redirecting him. God bless Geoffrey for his patience and teachings. How exciting it will be, he thought, to be able to tell Geoffrey that the mortgage would not be a problem any longer—that everything was again on track!

The new owners paid Sam the last installment and actually expressed great pleasure in their new home. Sam responded with pride: "And we thank you for the opportunity to serve and build for you. We have enjoyed this work. May you always find happiness here."

Sam paid each crewman and then the waiting Marcus, who was especially happy to see this completed home.

"I have partially cleared my land, Sam! I cannot tell you how excited my wife and I are to have our own home built at last. Not that we have not appreciated the King's generous lodgings within the castle's city walls . . . ," he reflected, "but my wife is a gardener, you see, and I have always wanted to raise goats."

"You mean you have not always dreamed of being in service to the King as a tax collector?" said Sam to this man who so rarely spoke of his personal life to any of the townspeople. And the minute he said it, Sam regretted his words.

"It is a good-paying job." Marcus's expression stiffened. "We all owe a duty to the King. How else can we staff the army, pave the roads, and have aqueducts built into the larger towns such as this one?"

"Of course, Marcus." Sam felt his heart sink. "Please forgive me. My attempt at humor was not well thought out. . . . Your position is indeed necessary, though I admit there are times I feel resentment. . . ." Sam felt himself stumbling over a moment that could have been a wonderful opportunity to ask Marcus about his hopes and dreams. He tried to regain ground. "But this is not what is important, is it? Today we start to plan your new home—a home that must be constructed to keep goats away from your wife's vegetables, yes?"

Sam felt better as Marcus managed a smile. "And this fine crew will create a home you will love!" Turning to face his crew, he was unexpectedly met with some embarrassed and sorrowful-looking faces—faces whose eyes would not meet his own. Again his heart sank.

"Men, surely you will agree to build Marcus's home—"

"Foreman Sam," began Thomas, "you mistake the reason for our great unease. We'd all like to work with you on this next project. But Grecco has assigned some of us—myself included—to another team. In fact, he assigned us several months ago—you didn't have contracts coming up and . . ."

Sam was quiet but calm. "I understand. But there are many who will build with me?" Sam looked at the men hopefully.

"Yes," replied Thomas. "But you need to speak to Grecco. Alone, Sam."

This time Sam felt his calm being replaced with anxiety. Still, he summoned his voice and announced, "Yes. Very well. I will go to see Grecco. Marcus, I will meet with you on Monday with a crew to begin your house! And to all these fine men standing here, I say thank you and God bless you! We have done what we set out to do. We have created a place where love can live. And this has been a good day!"

But with a heart full of doubts, he walked to the building site across town where Grecco was overseeing some repairs to the walls of the blacksmith's workshop.

. . .

"Sam! I was coming to see you at your home this evening." Grecco put out his hand to Sam.

As they shook, Sam responded. "Then I'm happy I've saved you a trip. My men said I was to speak with you. I'm hoping you are pleased with the many inquiries into my services for upcoming projects."

"I am pleased, Sam." Grecco motioned him to step aside to speak more privately. "But I must be forthright with you. I am releasing you from your foreman's duties for the next year. I'm putting you on John the Elder's crew. He's an excellent foreman with the same values you've demonstrated in building this last home. You'll agree with any decisions he makes, I'm sure, and I'm confident that he will learn from you too."

"I-I-I don't understand," stammered Sam, his cheery demeanor clouding over. "You're displeased with me . . . yet—"

Grecco put his hand on Sam's dejected shoulder. "I made this decision a few months ago, Sam. I wanted to wait until this last home was finished." Grecco's eyes were kind but adamant. "I think long and hard when I make decisions. I think about the work to be done, the customers, the crew, the financial effects, and I think about the effect my decisions will have on even one individual—such as yourself, Sam.

"For the past few years I have sadly observed your leadership skills worsen and your hastily built projects meet with growing dissatisfaction from customers. I've also watched your sense of worth become defined by your material possessions, and this has saddened me the most. I know what you are made of—I've loved you like a son, Sam, and I still believe in your talent and abilities—"

"Grecco. Please don't say this. I have recognized these same things! I've rededicated myself to God and I've changed my heart and my priorities. I've never felt more ready to lead than I do right now. . . ."

Grecco looked into Sam's imploring eyes and spoke slowly. "Then now is the perfect time for you to serve, Sam."

"Oh, Grecco, please believe me—"

"I do believe you. I see that you've turned your life around for the better. But I also know that a man can find it easy to change when he is at the mercy of God and His grace. The light is always more beautiful and uplifting to a man in search of a way out of the darkness. But will he follow that light in the glow of renewed success? *That* is the test of a man, Sam.

"Yes, I believe you. But your work still must speak for itself, and this last house will not erase the last few years. There are too many others who are hesitant about working for you or hiring you. You are defined by your habits and prevailing attitudes, not by one generous moment or one successful project. In fact, if I didn't love you as I do, and if there were not these recent requests for your services, I would actually be releasing you from the builders' guild altogether."

"But these requests. . . . I've made decisions based on these jobs. . . . At a crewman's pay, how will I live?" Sam could not help but feel overwhelming shame and a sense of failure. He shook his head from side to side and finally put his hands to his head.

"You may be more dependent on your past habits and perceptions of success, Sam, than you know. They take great effort and time to change. You wish to maintain your past lifestyle, even though it brought you misery?" Grecco paused, then returned to his firm stance. "You'll have to learn to live according to your means, as we all do. As a crewman you'll earn guaranteed wages every week. Surely that will offer some relief?" Grecco paused again, then again held out his hand to Sam. "Monday morning, you will meet with John's crew at the homesite of Marcus. I'll handle telling him about the change in foremen."

"Yes, Grecco. I'll be there."

. . .

At home, Suzette prepared a cup of tea for Sam as he sat in deep thought and prayer before the hearth fire. He was interrupted by a small, sweet voice.

"Daddy, why is your face so sad?"

A four-year-old child with a mop of curly dark hair took Sam's face between her two little hands and turned it toward her own serious face.

Sam managed a wan smile. "I'm not really sad, Mary. I'm praying to God and thinking very hard. I guess you could say I'm trying to figure out a . . . well, a problem."

"Can I help you, Daddy?" Little Mary cocked her head to one side, her eyes brightening with interest.

"No, my small child. You cannot." Then looking off, speaking more to himself, Sam added, "I'm afraid my past actions and attitudes have affected my future. I actually drove myself from my own work."

"You drove yourself where, Daddy?" The two insistent hands pulled Sam's face back around.

Sam took the hands, kissed them, and softly laughed. "Nowhere, honey. I guess you could say I was given the boot!" He smiled at Mary's solemn face.

Mary stared at her father's eyes. Then a spreading smile of glowing insight and hope broke out on her young face as she chirped happily, "Then you should go see Magowin!"

Sam was astonished. "Mary. . . . Why do you suggest this? What a helpful child! Why do you say I should go see Magowin the cobbler?"

Mary brimmed with pride at having helped her big, sad daddy. She stood straight before him and instructed, "So you can get the other boot!" . . .

And the next day . . .

. . . Sam and Magowin sat sharing a bowl of walnuts in the warm, familiar shoe shop.

"And I spoke without thinking to Marcus. I actually made fun of him, I think. How could I have done that? I thought my heart had changed. Instead I find that I have gone backward and have been assigned as a crewman until next autumn. Magowin, the joy and confidence I felt just two days ago have now escaped me. Why? Why this when I've pledged my love to God and to these laws of yours?"

Magowin cleared some shells from the bowl. "These are not my laws, good man."

"No, not yours. But these laws on how to live with true prosperity—where have they brought me? I put my heart and soul into my work. I felt fully alive—only to find that my past mistakes will shape my life? This shame I feel is too much for me." Sam's very soul was lost in despair. "I don't understand. I don't understand."

"And . . . you need to understand?"

Sam looked at Magowin. "Yes. I need to understand. I need to understand why God would allow this to happen to me when I have been praying and thanking Him for my new path, a new way of living, and for my . . . ha! My renewed prosperity! For this I must suffer such indignation? I have lost hope, Magowin."

"This is a sad statement," said the old cobbler. "But, my kind friend, these events do indeed reveal how the Divine works. Your attitude and reactions reveal less about God than they do about you. You trust your own perceptions on these matters so strongly that you feel justified in being angry at God? Hmm . . . yet you yourself admitted to concerns you had with holding on to your faith."

"What do you mean?"

"Do you remember after we took a load of wood in your cart to the young widow's house? After you had been talking to God in the forest? You came back a rich man that day, did you not? You had tapped into and experienced the wisdom of Divine Truth. You were filled with an amazing certainty that day—a glowing certainty. And you have experienced that same feeling at other moments along this new journey. And each time it buoys you, yes? It reminds you that God loves you and asks you to work with him through your honest dreams."

"Magowin, please. This only makes me think I have been foolish."

"Not foolish, Sam. Confused, perhaps. You misjudge your own thoughts. That day you asked me how you could hold on to this feeling and sure knowing—you said you were but a man with many faults. Do you remember asking me this?"

Sam sighed. "I remember."

"The answer is that you really cannot hold on to those wondrous moments of inspiration."

"But I thought . . ."

"Hmm. You thought. You thought that you could maintain control of this new spiritual path. You thought that you could feel safely wrapped in His communion always. You thought that you could stay aloft on your terms, released from material greed at last. You thought that by creating a new life open to divine inspiration, generosity, and love for others that you would escape anything you had created in the past."

"I don't understand. You said that if I followed the laws—"

"Yes. And you have, Sam. And God has rewarded you with the perfect circumstances to achieve your dreams."

"No, He hasn't!"

"Ah. Is that what *you* think, or what God thinks?"

"Magowin! How can I know what God thinks?"

"I'm so glad you asked!" Magowin sat back and smiled broadly. "We can never fully know what God thinks, but we can study what He teaches, we can learn from those who live by His teachings, and we can endeavor to shape our thoughts by His wisdom so that we begin to think as He does. You can only begin to know what God thinks by experiencing life with your soul, your heart, your eyes, your ears, and"—Magowin tapped his head—"and your mind open."

"I should have a mind that is open to being set back in my dreams?"

"That is *your* perception. *Your* reality. That is how *you* are choosing to analyze this development. My perception and reality and thoughts are not the same as yours."

"That's because you have not suffered this humiliation."

Magowin leaned forward and said quietly, "I have suffered through my own heartaches. I have endured things I would not wish on anyone. You have lost a foreman's position. I lost my Sarah—a fascinating woman with laughter like bells, a talent with cooking, and a trusting heart. For three long years I lost my will to follow God's urgings. For three long years I wallowed in a false reality. But for the faith of my dear wife, I would not have come out of that dark time. What she left behind lifted me back to hope. You are not alone in your sense of confusion." Magowin's eyes were wet with tears yet resolutely serene. The two men were silent for a long while.

"The reason my perception is different," Magowin continued, "is not that I am somehow holier than you, Sam, or because God loves me any differently. It is because I have spent many, many years allowing Him to live through me—and me through Him. I have allowed the Divine to shape my thoughts, my habits, my attitudes. My reality now permits what I once referred to as setbacks. Now I ask, 'What shall I learn from this?' I have faith, Sam. And that faith is rewarded with a miraculous, ever growing sense of understanding that is more satisfying than the head-spinning bursts of inspiration I feel when I fall to my knees in moments of divine revelation. You know what I mean by those moments?"

Sam was listening intently. "Yes. Moments when all is clear. When Truth fills your being. But I feel none of that now."

"Worry not. Those moments will continue to bless you in the future," smiled Magowin. "God knows how much we need them and how much they motivate us. But He also knows they cannot sustain us. He knows this very well."

"So where is He now? His presence seems to vanish. Even though I am following the laws and asking for His help."

"But you have yet to follow the fifth law."

"The fifth? I have failed after learning the first four!"

"No. You have not failed. That's *your* perception: *your* attitude, voice, mindset. *I* see this through clearer eyes."

Sam looked up, readying his hardened heart to hear a lecture on "seeing the best" in everything. But Magowin's wise, understanding eyes softened him and he found himself asking, "What do you see?"

"I see that your fine work on this last project saved you from being fired altogether. I see that you have been given all that you prayed for."

"No. Not all."

"Yes, all. You will still be in the building trade, and that is your dream, yes? You will still be loving others through your work, yes? And the best part is that for one whole year you can successfully budget and set upon wise financial planning because you'll know what your steady monthly earning will be."

"I can earn more as a foreman. . . ."

"You haven't lately."

"But I will—I could again."

"And slip back into the same habits of greed and anxiety?"

"No! I wouldn't. I've changed!"

"If you've changed, why does this upset you so?"

"You don't understand."

Magowin's voice became firm. "I *do* understand. What you're distressed about is your loss of position as foreman. Your loss of power, perhaps. Your dependence on this prestige will keep you from true success and freedom—and abundance. As long as you rely on a title or position for self-worth, you're no better off than when you relied on material accumulation. In your heart you know my words are true."

Sam eyed Magowin, searching his mind for a response. But he could find none. Everything Magowin said was true.

Very slowly, gently, Magowin continued. "You are not being punished. You think God can save you from consequences, but you have more creative power than you admit to. We all do. And you have created this consequence. Sadly, this was created before you turned back to God, but"—Magowin shrugged his shoulders—"that is how it is, so. . . . Go on.

"You have also helped to create a beautiful new house for folks who needed some love, and you've created a closer relationship with Suzette. That is good. Go on.

"You have felt the joy in giving. You have felt the energy that comes from loving your work and loving others. That is part of God's way. That is good. You have much to go forward on. And you have now a very wonderful thing. For deep inside you are praying fervently for understanding."

Sam whispered humbly, "Am I?"

"This despair. This pit. This frustration with God is actually a heartfelt prayer that is echoing through the halls of heaven as we speak." Magowin winked at Sam. "You are saying, 'Tell me why.' And He will, Sam. He will. You have advanced to the fifth law."

"How? I feel as though I've gone backward."

"Sometimes it does feel that way. Sometimes before a time of change—when we know our old habits and old ways of living and thinking will not work for us anymore—we do feel afraid and even angry. But it is at these times that growth is about to take place. This is your chance to think a whole new way. This is your chance to let go of the fear you have that others may see you as a crewman again and think, 'Aha! Once a wood gatherer, always a wood gatherer—'"

Sam turned pale, tears in his eyes. "Oh, Magowin. How . . . how do you know this? I could not even bear to speak it."

"Because I have love for you and I see you through God's eyes. And I have faith that you will see through God's eyes more and more and more. That is actually what you seek: understanding, Sam. The fifth law is the Law of Understanding. Understand your own fears and what is holding you back. You may believe in God's wisdom, you may prioritize, you may love others, and you may be generous . . . but until you are truly tested, you may not understand how your own attitudes and thoughts and mindset can be so very different from God's. This often comes as a despairing surprise to even the most religious folks I know, so don't be too hard on yourself. It can be an intimidating law, this Law of Understanding. It teaches that the goal of a successful life is to stay on a path that seeks to think and love and see as God thinks and loves and sees. Through ever increasing understanding, the believer experiences more wonder and more and more abundance."

"But that would take . . . forever."

"Precisely."

"That is the path of a holy man."

Magowin chuckled. "Heh! I like that!"

"I mean, it's the path of one who seeks no earthly riches, who requires no money. I must live as a worker. I am not like Pastor Wright who can spend his days in study and prayer. I have children and a home. I—I like this law, but surely a man such as I . . ."

"A man such as you is as beloved to God as anyone else He wants you to know Him. You need only begin and He will provide teachers and moments of inspiration your entire life. Your job is to understand when His thoughts have been made clear. Then you are to change: to think as He thinks—little by little." Magowin paused, thinking, then added brightly, "You are indeed a fortunate man, for the first step you will take toward this lifelong Law of Understanding is absolutely clear!"

"It is?"

"Oh, yes! You will learn to read." Magowin held up his hand as Sam began to protest. "You forget that I know a bit of how you think. No matter what you may say, I know why you have not learned. You thought you would appear to be a foolish woodsman. You thought you might fail. Better to stay the course than to fail! Hmm. . . . But to contemplate the holy writings in your own meditative silence, you must read. So . . . there you go. Pastor Wright will teach you. He can also direct you to other great writings that have been inspired by the mind of the Divine. Your world is about to open up, Sam. You will be in wonder and you will crave even more understanding. Plus Pastor Wright will also direct you to the sixth law."

"Pastor Wright? What is the sixth law?"

"The sixth law instructs that one must plan and set goals for personal and financial management."

"But, Magowin." Sam was taken aback. "I can imagine that Pastor Wright has much to teach me about spiritual matters, but not about money. What can a man who has so little money teach me about financial management?"

"Good question! You have opened yourself to another matter in which you require understanding!"

Sam groaned. "This is going to be a very long year."

"Ah! That reminds me!" Magowin jumped from his chair and, as sprightly as a young boy, he skipped back to the corner of his shop. "It is also going to be a cold, wet year, according to the widow Williams—and I find much wisdom from Mrs. Williams, I can tell you! So!" Magowin came back carrying a brand-new, superbly stitched pair of lined leather boots, freshly rubbed with oil. "These are for you—as payment for helping me last month. There will be days you must work in the damp. May they keep you warm and dry!" Magowin paused, puzzled. "Why are you laughing?"

All Sam could do was sputter between his hoots of joyful amazement. "Because—because you're so right, Magowin. There's much I have yet to understand, but if a four-year-old can teach me, then there's hope for me yet. There is hope."

11

Freedom

The next week was indeed cold and wet. Each day Sam walked the mile to Marcus's new homesite—wearing his new, sturdy work boots—and reported to John the Elder. And each day Sam and the other tradesmen wondered if they would be sent home due to the weather conditions. But they were not sent home.

It is a happy man indeed who can turn a wet, slushy day into a creative opportunity—and John was such a man. With good humor every morning, John announced to the crew that the weather would not permit much timber work, yet would not deter their progress. "We're going to divide into two crews while it rains. One crew will gather stones from the creek bed on the property, and sort them for either chimney or wall building. The other will dig out rocks from the garden site, terrace the beds, lining them with rocks so that the disturbed soil won't wash away. If it keeps raining, we'll finish the terracing, watching where the rainwater flows, and construct runoff channels, to keep the gardens from collecting too much water. During breaks when the skies are clear, we'll work on the house. But there is much we can do, even in this drizzle!"

On the third day of terracing and garden preparation, a mason offered, "But, sir, I've wielded a pick for three days now. Are we contracted to create these gardens? We are not landscapers, we're builders."

"We are more than builders of buildings. We're builders of homes and dreams," John countered with enthusiasm. "We know that Marcus's wife plans to garden, do we not? We know that the home will have a hearth and chimney, do we not? We also know that staying home can only delay our progress—and our pay! Therefore, by unearthing and gathering all these stones, we save them money on brick for the chimney. By preparing these beds, we know that crops will be grown—for us to later buy and enjoy! Plus we know we are delighting our customers! Why, then, would we stay home and miss these opportunities?"

Sam listened and nodded. Grecco was correct. This was a foreman whose heart was in his work and whose instruction was valuable and uplifting to Sam. In his new boots, in his "new" position, with a new heart, Sam glowed in the misty gray days that saw Marcus's homesite turn into a gardener's paradise.

After two weeks' time, the gardens were complete, a foundation had been constructed, and timbers had been hewn. Marcus and his wife wept silent tears when they saw the wonderful beds and garden sections that had been laid out. "John," asked Marcus quietly, "are we to pay extra for all this work? We do not have—"

"No. The contract remains the same, Marcus. We have saved quite a bit by ordering no brick. I was hoping a stone hearth and chimney would be suitable. . . ."

"Yes. Oh, yes!" Marcus replied.

"Very well, then. Just reward us next year with turnips and berries!" John smiled broadly and turned back to his work.

. . .

Sam sat across from Suzette that evening with his two weeks' wages on the table. "This is all I will be bringing home each fortnight. It's not much. . . ."

"It's plenty," replied Suzette. "We'll live very well on these wages along with my income."

"And we will tithe. . . ."

"Of course. Always."

"Then we will need to . . ." Sam paused.

Suzette placed her hands on Sam's. "We will finally get to live in the cozy little home of our dreams. The one on the market square that I've always adored—you know, the one with the large shuttered window in the front. It is going to be sold soon. Sam, surely we can sell this large house and find happiness in that beautiful cottage. I see us there, Sam. I have always seen us there in the bustling town center, where folks can pass by and smell my gooseberry pies cooling in the window."

"And view your curtains and dresses and cloth ware," Sam added with a knowing, loving smile.

Suzette returned his smile. "It would be a perfect home for us."

"The house is to be sold? The widow Williams? She has not taken ill, has she?"

"Not at all! She is to be married again! Magowin has proposed. Isn't that wonderful?"

Sam listened in peaceful amazement. Instead of feeling devastated about giving up this fine, expensive house, Suzette was alit with hope and excitement. And he, too, felt calm and happy—with a secure understanding that prayers were being answered all around him.

"That is blessed news. Blessed, blessed news. And it is a lovely home. I will talk to Geoffrey tomorrow about selling this house—after I take our tithe to Pastor Wright," Sam replied, reflecting on Magowin's instruction.

. . .

"I've brought a contribution to the church's work, Pastor Wright." Sam handed over a small pouch of coins. "Suzette tells me the reading classes are under way and going well."

"Bless you! Thank you! Come in, my man. Come in, Sam. Share these biscuits and fresh butter with me!" Pastor Wright led him into a small study with walls lined with books and papers. It smelled of old bindings and yellowing paper—the comforting, intriguing smell of ancient knowledge and inspiring thoughts and stories.

"Your family has added much to this church and community, Sam. Suzette has started a class for the younger readers, and I have the older children. Your daughter Martha helps with the youngest children—she's so like a little lady, isn't she? Your tithes are invaluable. We are richly blessed. We have purchased desks and many, many books and tablets already."

"So much?" Sam was pleasantly amazed.

"Pastor Wright smiled. "I am very careful with budgeting, and good at finding bargains. I have to be! But here, try this biscuit."

Sam sat, enjoying this warm room and delicious buttery biscuit. Taking in the vast number of volumes around him—volumes filled with age-old wisdom and new ideas, volumes filled with information and history, volumes filled with philosophy and poetry—he knew that now was the time to admit one of the dreams of his heart.

"Ahem . . ." started Sam. "I was wondering, Pastor. . . . Well, I was wondering if you might instruct me on how to—"

"Develop a financial plan?" Pastor Wright quickly offered.

Sam was stuck on a reply. "I . . . no . . . pardon me? What made you say that?"

"Oh, I advise and guide many couples and single people on sound financial planning and money management. It's part of my job."

"Your job?"

"Certainly! The spiritual well-being of every parishioner is my utmost concern. And I know that poverty and lack of financial priorities and planning contribute to great unhappiness and sidetracked values."

"So you teach financial management?"

"Heavens, yes! It's imperative, don't you think?"

"Well, yes, but what do *you* know . . . what I mean is, how do people believe that you—living on so little income—can give advice on financial matters?"

"Could there be a better person? The fact that I live quite

happily within my means should offer proof that it can be done. Yes, it surely can be done. And in case you are saying to yourself, Sam, that it is my position as a minister that enables me—directs me—to have a financially disciplined, content, and generous spirit, I will give you something to think about. Perhaps it is instead my disciplined, contented, and generous spirit that led me to my job."

Sam listened, thinking about this man in a new light.

"Do you know why I wish to teach children to read?" the pastor went on. "Because they will find greater happiness and closeness to God when they can read His words. Do you know why I teach people to budget and plan? Because they will find greater happiness and closeness to God when they are free to follow their calling without the restraints of debt, material greed, and financial confusion. If my parishioner is a poor man, but he finds happiness—true happiness—in his work, he must still budget and tithe and save. He may have very little materially, but he will be rich in spirit, just as my wealthy parishioner must also practice sound financial planning. Sometimes it is the wealthy man who is in need of the most instruction, for his resources are a responsibility and he is easily chained by them. But he, too, can and must find freedom in order to walk more closely with God."

"You are so right. Of course you are right, but I had no idea that this was part of your . . . your . . ."

"My mission."

Sam was struck by the seriousness in Pastor Wright's youthful eyes. "We are fortunate to have you in our town, Pastor."

Pastor Wright leaned back. "I know that you have taken a well, a new position with John the Elder, and I thought perhaps you might need a bit of instruction on money matters." Pastor Wright looked intently into Sam's eyes. "Some planning and preparation guidance. It's only natural."

Sam felt a cool, easy breath go in and out of his mind and body. "I do need your instruction, Pastor Wright. But not because I'm in a mess. Rather, Suzette and I are starting upon a very joy-filled path. We already know that we will sell our home, so we will not have that financial burden. I am committed to my work, no matter what position I may hold. Suzette is committed to her work. We are committed to our children. And we are committed to God, the source of our strength. We are blessed to find the joy in tithing and giving. And we will use our money wisely and not make mistakes that we made—that I made—in the past. I took part in foolish investments and purchased much on credit. I am very good at handling a budget for a building project, but . . ."

"But when it comes to your own finances, you don't have short- or long-term goals and plans?"

"No. Not really. And I know I should—we should—but . . ."

"*Why* should you?"

"What do you mean?"

"I want to know why you think you should study and practice financial preparation and planning."

"So that I live within my means and avoid debt, of course."

Pastor Wright scrunched his face. "What drudgery! Surely there is a more exciting reason!"

"Pastor Wright! You are confusing me, just as Magowin does sometimes!"

"Magowin! That character! He came by to see me the other day!"

"To ask you about a wedding ceremony?" Sam smiled.

"There are no secrets in this town. Yes! He is to marry again! What a happy occasion that is going to be. He is a beloved man . . . a special cobbler. Aren't we lucky he makes our shoes?"

"Of course! He's very good"—Sam smiled—"and always generous."

"Precisely! Magowin makes the effort to live well below his means so that he is able to make his living as a cobbler . . . a cobbler with enough free time to attend to those in need and minister to those who seek his counsel. Without strict financial planning and budgeting, this could never have been possible. Do you know that?"

"I have not inquired into his finances, Pastor Wright."

"What I mean is this: Do you know that without strict financial preparation you cannot freely live your dreams—responsibly and completely?"

"Yes, I know that. That's what I said before, isn't it?"

"Not really. You said that you should adhere to financial preparedness and planning to enable you to live within your means and avoid debt."

Sam was silent again. Slowly he began. "I do know what you are saying. You are saying that living within my means and avoiding debt are not my actual goals. My actual plan is to walk with the Divine through this life and to put my heart, mind, and energy into work that I love. My plan is to enjoy and love my family and live with a loving, generous spirit. These are my plans and goals. To stay on my course, I must live within my means and avoid debt—not because these are final goals, but because they will enable me to breathe freely and enjoy life."

Now Pastor Wright was silent. "Amen, my brother. You are more in tune than many parishioners. You are already on this path. I will not need to start with the first law of highest prosperity with you, I see."

Sam straightened up. "Magowin has been enlightening me on these laws. Pastor Wright, you are a spiritual minister, so you will understand these words." Sam paused to collect his thoughts. "When I first walked into Magowin's shop, I was filled with anxiety and a desire for money. I wasn't even there to see Magowin. I was there seeking the whereabouts of Geoffrey. I was consumed with the fear of losing my grip on prosperity—for you see I once did earn quite a bit of money. . . ."

"And you probably will again," Pastor Wright added.

"But that's just it, Pastor Wright. Now I understand that wealth is not the beginning of happiness. These laws—the Seven Laws of Highest Prosperity that Magowin teaches and lives by—these are really laws on how to live with a full heart and how to find prosperity within the arms of God. I walked into Magowin's shop seeking financial help to fill my emptiness. I sit before you now, a man who knows that money can never fill that void. I sit before you, a man who looks forward to a life that I create with God. I wish to seek the understanding and wisdom of God, not financial riches."

"Hmm. . . . You are at the fifth law," mused the pastor. "Of course, you know this divine understanding is a lifelong quest —a life-filling, soul-filling, longstanding openness to God's will and His ways."

"I do know this and that is actually why I am here. Magowin suggested that I learn to read. I cannot ask Suzette to teach me: I know how frustrated I will be, and I—"

"Say no more. I understand. This is not unusual. When you finish with your first reading lessons, you may feel more comfortable in asking for her instruction."

"Then you will agree to teach me?"

"That would be an absolute pleasure! Not only will you learn to read, but I will have the opportunity to discuss great thoughts and questions with you—for you see, I too am constantly seeking and learning the Divine's ways, and sharing with others magnifies the Light by which we all learn. But I must also ask that you allow me to instruct you on financial preparedness."

"Well, yes, Pastor Wright, but surely by selling our home and reducing our expenses, we are showing that we are prudent with our money. I will not get into the same trouble I did before. I know this because I will not be tempted. I am finding that I am content to serve. There is no shame in working on John the Elder's crew. I have come to understand that peace and happiness are more important than wealth. I am looking forward to a simpler life. My wife and children are in agreement. I feel content about my future. If we are wise with our finances and continue to tithe and enjoy giving, why would we need to study financial management? Money is no longer my focus."

"You feel content about your future?"

"Yes, Pastor Wright." Sam beamed.

"But not particularly excited. . . ."

"Excited? Well . . . in a way, I suppose. Suzette is excited, this I know."

"I wonder why. . . . Because she will be leading a simpler life?"

Sam laughed. "I'm not sure of that. Suzette stays very busy. She is truly alive when she is embroidering and stitching, and she somehow manages to attend to the home and children . . . more so than I—"

"*And* teach a reading class."

"And teach, yes. She has always taught the children and even neighbor children, at times. I cannot see how her life will be simpler. In fact, I think she likes Mrs. Williams's house because it has a large window that opens onto the market square. My wife is a businesswoman, you know—"

"One of the best," added the pastor. "How much better our town would be if all approached their work with the same care and love. Hmm. . . . I would not be surprised if Suzette had bigger dreams for her seamstress business. Especially now that the children are older and your eldest daughter, Martha, can watch the other two at times."

Sam's eyes twinkled. "You do know my wife well."

"And I know you, Sam."

"Me? In what way?"

"I know that you have dreams of a brighter future."

"I did, Pastor Wright, but I am no longer interested in status or wealth. Truly I am not. That is why I would not be a very good financial student. I would prefer to study the wisdom of God and spend more time in prayer. I am content to serve and gain understanding."

"So you would deprive this town of your gifts?"

"Pastor Wright! Of course not! No matter how small our income, we will continue to tithe and continue to help those in need. And I will always serve through my work as a crewman."

Pastor Wright looked intently at Sam. "Your words have a noble sound. But I want to hear what your heart is saying. Do you truly feel that you have become the person you dreamed of being?"

Sam paused. "So much has happened in the last few months, Pastor, that this is difficult to answer. I do know that I never again want to live without listening to God's voice. I do know that I want to understand and follow His ways. Is this what I dreamed of? I think so. For, whenever I have felt lifted and inspired, I now know that God was with me. When I turned my attention to material possessions and envy and greed, I walked without inspiration. I was empty inside." Sam looked into his hands. "So, yes, this is who I always dreamed of being, because I am with God."

"You are telling me that once you became prosperous and successful, you left God out of the picture?"

"Yes, I know I did."

"So you associate success and prosperity with unhappiness and emptiness?"

Sam laughed softly. "Now I do. I certainly did not always feel that way."

"You can be one of the best foremen in this town, Sam, don't you agree?"

A great heaviness fell upon Sam and crept into his voice. "Pastor Wright, I cannot think about such matters. I thought I could not bear to face God again, but I did. I thought I could not feel great love for others, but I now do. I thought I could not humble myself before a cobbler or before my wife and then to my crew—but I did, and I was strengthened for this. I thought I could not bear the humiliation of stepping down from a job I loved—but I have found peace and understanding these last two weeks. I thought my house and possessions defined me, but I am freed from that burden. I have always been afraid to learn to read—to ask to be taught—but here I am asking and you have agreed to instruct me. There is so much I am now free to do, Pastor. Why do you ask me about old dreams? I am no longer a foreman, and that is as it should be. I finally feel free. I am content. Financial success no longer interests me."

"So you don't intend to listen to God?"

Sam was aghast. "What do you mean?"

"Was it not God who opened your heart to possibilities and dreams? Was it not the Divine Spirit who filled you with the love and foresight to lead your crew to build such a lovely house last month? When you finished that house, did you praise God at all?"

"Yes, I did. I felt He was there with us. My heart was filled every day . . . but that has changed. Now I am happy to serve John the Elder. He, too, brings wisdom and love to his work. I am free of status and prestige."

"You are afraid."

"I'm not afraid. I am calm and resigned to my role as an honorable worker. As long as I live within my means, what does it matter if I am not a foreman?"

"You are afraid, Sam."

"I just got *over* being afraid. How can you say I'm afraid?"

"You are afraid to again follow your dreams and become a successful foreman and builder. In fact, you probably had dreams of leading a new guild of builders, to assign your own foremen."

"I'm not afraid, Pastor. I'm just wiser. I know where all that leads."

"No. You know where it led before."

"And why would it not be different if I had such ambitions again?" Sam asked with some indignation.

"Because you are different."

Sam shook his head wearily. "It is too much for me to dream of this again."

"You are afraid."

Sam sighed deeply. "I am not prepared to follow such dreams again."

"Spiritually prepared? Physically?" asked Pastor Wright.

"I'm not prepared to handle the financial responsibility. I'm afraid that I will fall back into an emptiness if I—" Sam stopped when he heard his words. He leaned back and closed his eyes.

"Sam! This is no time to become weary! This is great news! You are ready for the sixth law—and you know that you are ready!"

Sam opened his eyes and searched the pastor's face. "But I am safe now. I know there are seven laws, but surely a man such as I does well to work and live by the first five laws."

"You were not born to be safe, Sam. You can, indeed, live with some honor by following the first five laws. You would bring honor to your trade no matter what your job title. This I believe, Sam. But you are not here to bring honor to your trade. You're here to bring honor to the life that God has created." Pastor Wright paused. "When you use the talents that God gives you, you honor Him and you honor life. When your work serves God and others, as well as your own heart, you will find yourself with more financial rewards. And you are to prepare for this, Sam. There is no shame in preparing for success."

"I prepared for success before."

"No. You did follow your heart, and you advanced in your work, but then you became paralyzed by success—or your ideas of success. You were not prepared because you had not established a plan that included the giving, spending, and saving habits that hold true no matter what your income. Plus you began investing without a plan and with no guidance. You lost money and you lost hope. Strange how those are so closely tied, eh?" Pastor Wright shot Sam an inquisitive yet wise glance.

"But I'm giving now, and I'm reducing my spending."

"That is good, but the Law of Preparation calls for much, much more. You must know what you are actually preparing for, Sam. You must rediscover the fire within you to create and work the way you know you can. And you must admit to yourself that foolish money management has and can destroy that dream. You must start now, no matter how small your income, to follow the simple steps of sound financial planning.

Then those habits will stay with you as you pursue a leadership role—once again—in your craft. You must prepare mentally and financially for any setback, for as you know, there are lean times in your line of work. But if this is your true work, then you can prepare for those lean times and still live with a joyful and fulfilled heart."

"These steps are simple?" Sam asked cautiously.

Pastor Wright grinned slowly. "Well, sure! All you have to do is give ten percent, save twenty percent, and do a detailed budget to live on the remainder—considering expenses such as home repairs, livestock, tools for your business, unforeseen illness, any advanced schooling your daughters may warrant, perhaps their weddings, your own later years when you will want to enjoy your grandchildren . . ."

"Wait. Wait. Those aren't simple steps!" protested Sam.

"Sure they are! They are much simpler than the alternative—no planning and no formula, which leads to . . . well, you know where that leads! Unless you plan and prepare a path, you will never find lasting freedom. And it's amazing how a desire for freedom can make a sacrifice seem a simple choice. If you were preparing for only a balanced budget, these steps would seem tedious and difficult. But if you are preparing for a life of significance, doing the work you love, helping the community, enjoying your family, and praising God, then these are not tedious steps. They are a formula for the freedom to pursue that life."

Sam's heart and eyes began to glow with renewed dreams. "You think I can learn how to manage my finances? Even if I find myself with greater wealth again?"

"I believe with all my heart that this is so, because you are on a path with God's guidance and your heart is ready to see money as a tool, not a goal."

Sam breathed slowly. "Please teach me to prepare for greater prosperity, Pastor Wright. Because you are right. I do want to be the foreman of my own crew again, and I do want to achieve more in life—to offer my ideas, my workmanship, my leadership. My greatest joy was working with earnest love for the project, my crew, and the customers. I felt alive, and my family benefited also. But I do know that this can bring greater commissions and greater risks. I want the inner peace that I can manage all the responsibilities that come with such a life."

"Praise to God! What a gift you give me—to ask me to teach you! For this is my passion! I know that you must go to visit Geoffrey. Go, then, and settle this matter with him. He will help you, I know, for Geoffrey is quite intelligent when it comes to investments and money matters. He and I . . . well, let's just say we have been teaching each other many things this past year. Then go home and have a fine supper with Suzette and your children. After services tomorrow, we will talk about our preparation sessions, yes? For there will be many. We will divide them between reading lessons and financial matters. Letters and figures! Ha! I have much to teach you! What fun we will have! You are indeed preparing for a greater life ahead."

And so he was.

Sam worked out a mutual arrangement with Geoffrey: Their prestigious house on Miller Street was sold to a pharmacist. Magowin and the widow Williams were united in a joyful wedding. And Sam and Suzette did indeed purchase and move into the little house in the town center. They sold off some furnishings and paid off some debts. After much discussion and a few family meetings, their three daughters became more agreeable to sharing one room. Their "new" older home began to smell of gooseberry pies, vegetable stews, and fresh bread.

Sam's life was again on track . . . but his life was not easy. Sam had been through many hardships in his life, but he was not prepared for how difficult the "simple" steps of reading—and the "simple" steps of giving, saving, and budgeting—would be.

At their first reading lesson, Sam realized how slowly he would learn and how frustrating this instruction would be.

But Pastor Wright insisted that all the frustration would have a blessed result. Stopping their first lesson, Pastor Wright stood Sam before his large library of books.

"Your actual assignment is to read all these books," he said—with a confident, calm expression.

"B-b-but," stammered Sam. "It will never be possible! I'm just learning the letters and sounds. . . . To read all these great books. . . . Why, that would take the rest of my life!"

"What a splendid answer! You could have said 'I'll never be able to read all these!' If this will take you the rest of your life, isn't it best we get back to work?"

And so they did. At each lesson, the pastor read from the Scriptures and wise texts, and together they discussed philosophy and theology, poetry, and the human condition. This encouraged Sam all the more to learn to read proficiently on his own—he had a grander goal than reading. Reading was just part of the preparation process, although it was certainly difficult and he needed faith and discipline. He kept his eyes on his real goal—there was study and learning to do. And how these subjects filled his heart and mind!

Every Tuesday and Thursday at five o'clock Sam met with Pastor Wright for reading lessons, which went very, very slowly. And every Tuesday and Thursday at six he reviewed and revised his meager budget to comply with the rules of wise money management. The first 10 percent went to God's work. The next 20 percent went to savings. But the remaining 70 percent was torturously difficult to budget, and Sam needed much reinforcement and encouragement from Pastor Wright every week to keep saving 20 percent, even though Sam thought he needed more of their income for daily purchases.

Sam and Suzette had thought they could barely live on 90 percent of their income. And here Pastor Wright was saying they must save 20 percent and live on 70 percent? How many times did he and Suzette yearn to buy a beautiful rug or piece of pottery, only to admit that it would cut into their savings plan? How many times did Suzette in frustration serve turnip soup for days on end because they refused to spend more than the allotted amount on groceries out of their remaining 70 percent? How difficult it was to give up the milk delivery in order to pay just a bit less at the market! And how difficult it was to hand taxes over to Marcus every two weeks!

Sam and Suzette could have allowed themselves to feel poor. Yet somehow . . . somehow they did not. They were wealthy in spirit and hope. They cheerfully attended to their work (on most days)! They gave and saved as if they were wealthy. After a few months, they found that their sacrifices and disciplined ways were creating more than a comfortable savings—they were creating feelings of peace and a freedom from want and need. To their amazement, they found that they could live on very little and began to enthusiastically see money as a tool that they could control. Sam's time with Pastor Wright became devoted less to financial planning and budgeting matters, and more to reading and study.

Sam continued to work with John the Elder, bringing home little pay but a great deal of optimism for the life he was preparing to lead. Marcus's house was completed and within six months, Marcus's wife was shooing baby goats out of her bountiful, rock-terraced gardens. More building and repair projects had kept John's crew busily working—and whistling—throughout the winter and into the following summer.

But as Sam worked, he did more than whistle. He prayed and planned in his head what his projects would be when he would once again lead his own crew. For he knew that his life's work was not to simply cut and shape timbers, or dig and lay stone. His life's work would be—as it always had been—to think, create, build, and lead in a new, productive way. And he was working toward this—living on a limited income, but saving every penny that he could in preparation for greater work ahead.

12

Making a Trail

Sam stood with Grecco in the shade of a generous oak tree a year after Sam's demotion.

"I have been watching you, Sam. Your workmanship is excellent, of course, and your dedication is obvious. John the Elder has repeatedly expressed to me that you are a gifted worker and builder. He has asked me several times why I have not promoted you again to foreman of one of my crews."

Sam looked straight at Grecco. "And now I present myself to you, Grecco. I am eager to lead a crew once more. Not for the status—"

Grecco put a hand on Sam's shoulder. "I understand. I have been watching more than your work. Your heart is renewed. I know of your tithes and Suzette's work with the school. I know of your own studies. I know of your amazing thrift. Did you know you are one of the few crewmen in town to have an account with the banker?" Grecco winked at Sam. "I need a man like you to lead these crewmen."

"I am ready," offered Sam.

"There will be few jobs at first."

"I have savings I can live on."

"Oh, that won't be necessary. You can still work on John's crew between your assignments. Unless, of course, that would disgrace you." Grecco eyed Sam.

Sam smiled. "God's unfailing grace fills my life and my heart. I accept this offer. I feel no shame in stepping down from foreman between commissions to serve with John."

. . .

And so it was that Sam was once again given the opportunity to lead a crew—a small crew—as small as his very first crew eight years before. He was assigned to minor projects and repair jobs. His crew became accustomed to his approach. Roofs were thatched, stone was laid, framework was anchored, and even drainage tiles were repaired with care and love for those whose lives would be touched by their work. Between assignments Sam worked for John, but these times became fewer as more customers requested Sam and more men came to work for him. His pay increased, his tithes increased, his savings increased, and his faith and understanding increased. But his goals were so clear and his budgeting habits were by now so natural, that his spending increased only for small luxuries—milk and cheese delivery, more fruits and finer cuts of meat—which Suzette was quite willing to accept!

Life was truly invigorating. He looked forward to work every day. His crew looked forward to work—for they knew it was important work that they were doing. After all—they were working for Sam! Suzette's sewing business kept her almost too busy at times. Pastor Wright's school continued to be blessed with Suzette's teaching and the small rooms were filled with students. Suzette and Sam's daughters, Martha, Elizabeth, and Mary, were helpful and happy learners. And he too was an ardent student. Life was a joy. Sam was energized and enthusiastic, spiritually and emotionally at peace, and confident that Suzette and he were truly financially secure . . .

until one day . . .

. . . when Sam took his small mortgage payment to Geoffrey. The lender greeted him warmly, then motioned for him to step inside.

"I have an urgent matter to discuss with you, Sam."

"Of course, Geoffrey."

The two men sat down with a pot of tea between them. In the quiet, austere room, Geoffrey's soft words came like thunder in the distance. "You are a builder. You are a good builder. But there is something that you have built that is wearing away, bit by bit. It is crumbling as we sit here. You are in danger of losing much if you do not attend to this."

Sam was puzzled. "What? Pray tell me this is not so! What can you mean?" Sam searched his mind. Had he constructed anything for Geoffrey? Was his own house not sound? Was there a fence, a wall . . . ? "Geoffrey, I will repair whatever it is. Tell me."

"I am speaking of your savings."

Sam blinked at Geoffrey. Then he smiled. "You are a thoughtful man to be concerned about my finances, Geoffrey, but we have been very frugal and we have managed to save quite a bit. You need not worry about us. For the past year we have tithed, just as you instructed, and still we save twenty percent of our income. We have no debt other than our small mortgage. There is no danger of my finances going to ruin as they did before."

Geoffrey listened quietly, patiently nodding. "This is wise, indeed. And you are now more prosperous?"

"I still do not earn what I once did, but yes, I am a richly blessed man. I've been faithful to the laws of highest prosperity, Geoffrey. My strength is God's grace and wisdom, my priorities are spiritually guided. I feel blessed to share, and now I cannot imagine myself other than as one who gives gladly."

"Yes. It is wonderful to let your money bring happiness to others, isn't it?"

"It has become part of who we are, Suzette and me—part of our walk on this path with our Creator. And this fills us with awe. You opened our eyes and hearts to being generous, and I thank you."

"God opened your eyes and hearts. I was the messenger. You were ready to hear the words."

"He always seems to know when I'm ready," Sam added humbly. "He opened my ears to Suzette's guidance, and now I put love into all my work. I seek every day to understand the thoughts and ways of God. And I am prepared to face challenges. My goals and thoughts are clear. And . . ." Sam beamed. "And we have built up four thousand royal gold coins in the bank! So you see, Geoffrey, you need not worry about my financial security."

"Oh, but I do worry, my good man. I am very concerned. Tell me. . . . Do you know what a pound of tea cost a year ago?"

Sam paused. "I couldn't say. . . ."

"It cost around sixteen farthings. How about a cord of fine wood?"

"Last year? About eleven farthings. But that was last year."

"And this year?"

"It is now about eleven farthings and half."

"And I just bought tea at close to seventeen farthings," Geoffrey said wistfully.

"This is always so. Each year costs go up a little, but wages are usually raised, so . . . this has no great effect, yes?" Sam offered casually.

"It has effect, to be sure." Geoffrey poured two cups of tea. "If you had eleven hundred farthings last year, Sam, and you bought ten cords of fine wood to store in your shed, how much would it be worth today?"

"If it was kept dry, why . . . I could sell it for today's price. Eleven and half a cord, so eleven hundred fifty farthings."

"And would you have actually made money?"

"Hmm. Not really, I suppose," said Sam. "For, that eleven-fifty wouldn't buy any more goods than my eleven hundred farthings could have purchased last year. Is that your point?"

"Yes. Good. Now let us say that last year you didn't buy wood with your eleven hundred farthings. Let's say that, instead, you wisely saved it in the bank. . . ."

"Oh, then I would make money. I earn three percent annual interest on my deposits."

"And after a year that would be . . ."

Sam did some quick figuring. "Eleven hundred thirty-three farthings at the end of . . . one year."

"And if you were to take that saved money out, could you again buy ten cords of wood at today's price?"

"I wouldn't have quite enough. My money would have—"

"Lost value, Sam."

Sam's eyes narrowed as he took this in.

"My four thousand gold coins . . ."

"Will actually be worth less in a year. The prices of goods have been going up about five percent a year for as long as I have been tracking them. Some items go down in cost, but that is rare. You need to have a five-percent increase in salary just to stay even. And your stored money needs to earn five percent in order to maintain its value. Do you see this?"

"Yes, but the bank pays three percent. Surely that's better than storing my coins in my house—earning no interest," Sam said thoughtfully.

"To be sure, my good man, and you do need to be saving. This twenty percent that you put aside is wise and proper, according to the Law of Preparation. And you are correct; it's better than storing the coins in your house. But heed my words well. If you keep storing all your savings in this safe three-percent-interest-bearing account, it will slowly erode over time. At the end of twenty to twenty-five years, when you are ready to live off your savings, you will have a large sum of money to be sure, but it will have lost quite a bit of real value as prices will have increased. You are setting your money aside, and you are indeed saving it because you are not spending it. But in no way are you preserving your money."

"Geoffrey, this is disheartening. Should I put my money in a different bank? Is there one that pays five percent interest?"

"There are other places to store your money, yes, but you are ready to move beyond mere savings, Sam. You're ready to start investing so that your money creates more money for you."

"Oh, no. . . ." Sam leaned back. "I invested a few years ago. I lost money, I didn't make any. These businessmen promised huge returns, and I believed them. But the businesses I invested in failed, and so did my investments."

"I understand," said Geoffrey, so quietly that Sam strained to hear. "But there are many ways to invest that are neither as risky nor as ill-advised. It is my business to know how to get money working and earning money. I can guide you. You do agree that you must preserve that which you've saved for the future?"

"Yes! Oh, yes," replied Sam.

"And you do know that money well invested will allow your money to grow and work for you."

Sam sipped on his tea, in thought. Then he looked up and shook his head. "Of this I am not convinced. Or should I say, I'm not sure I need to involve myself in such matters. I'm not a greedy man."

At this, Geoffrey leaned back, smiled with warmth at Sam, and then began to chuckle good-naturedly, taking Sam by surprise. He had never heard Geoffrey laugh before.

"My good man, earning a higher return and preserving or even increasing your wealth does not make you greedy. I am not laughing at you, Sam, but at myself, I suppose. Seeking a higher return to preserve or increase your wealth is not a greedy venture. Greed stems from motive. Would you be greedy if you wanted to send Martha to a teacher's school someday, and you needed a higher return on your savings in order to do so?"

"Well, no. . . . I suppose not," said Sam.

"Would you be greedy if you realized that Suzette could never live off your savings in the event of your death—and you decided instead to invest in order to increase your wealth?"

Sam frowned. "If I had the right investments, then . . . perhaps that investment would be fair and not greedy."

"I agree, Sam, that you are not a greedy man. If you were, I would not be sharing tea with you on this fine autumn day trying to convince you to save your crumbling savings. I have little patience with greedy men. For you see, I was once the greediest man in all the shire." Geoffrey paused to sip his tea. And then he told his tale.

He told of how, not unlike Sam, he had grown up with meager means and a yearning heart. He learned at a young age of his gift for the workings of money, and he tapped into this gift wholeheartedly. Instinctively knowing which people, which products, which businesses would flourish or fail, he supported those showing promise. He became thrilled at the dividends he earned when profits rolled in. Soon he was charging fees, as well, for advising others on how to invest.

Watching money turn into more money was a passion for him. His every working hour was spent in studying and graphing the various markets—the price of wheat, the price of chickens, the price of wool—and seeking information from those who, in turn, were students of the natural world. The weather, the temperature, the stars, the grasshopper numbers, the felling of trees . . . all had an eventual affect on crops and the wants and needs of people. He studied these shifts. He studied the progress of the King's projects, and the royal court's wants and needs, and the taxes required. Everything, he discovered, affected the prices and values of commodities. And this man Geoffrey was by far the most shrewd, keen observer, student, and adviser on investing in all the land.

When a fire raged though a forest in a distant area of the realm, he stockpiled local lumber to sell at a premium the following season. When the King doubled taxes to build new roads, Geoffrey pulled his share of money from the town's new jewelry business, then opened his own back door to buy gems, gold, and silver from those in need of money. These precious goods he then sent to a foreign country to be sold at great profit. All was legal. All was business. And the business was creating money—in order to make more. It could certainly be done, and it could certainly be done well.

Even the bankers sought Geoffrey's advice and, after a while, Geoffrey realized he had more to gain monetarily in refusing to divulge his knowledge and plans and actions. Instead he offered only shares in his fund of money. Geoffrey would make 12 percent and turn over 8 percent to those who secured their money with him. His assets and wealth increased substantially.

When the markets and opportunities grew flat, he turned to lending money for mortgages and businesses that he knew might fail. But the human effect of such a failure was not his concern. His concern was that, until the loan failed, he would earn interest. Then, when the borrower could not pay, Geoffrey took control of the collateral, always at a bargain price. The object was to create money—that was it. Nothing more. And so . . . money was all he did create. Greed consumed him and he produced nothing of any real or lasting value.

"For twenty-five years," Geoffrey recounted, "my methods earned me a great deal of money. A great deal. But I was an empty man, no longer passionate. I grew bored with life. To try to fill my emptiness, I charged the highest rates I could—what the market would bear, as they say. I cared little about the borrowers' motives or whether they truly had the means to pay. I gave no thought to making loan after loan to the same people who became buried in debt to me." Geoffrey paused and looked with humility at Sam. "I permitted you to take out a loan for a house on Miller Street—That was five years ago. An eternity ago—I knew you were in over your head, but I set up that huge mortgage. . . . I could never do that today."

Sam was transfixed. He knew that Geoffrey was a man of means because he was able to lend money. But he did wonder why his furnishings were so modest. Hesitantly he asked, "Did you . . . lose it all? What I mean is . . . what changed?"

"I had dealings with a man named Menro."

"I know that man!" Sam sat up straight. "I stayed in his stables when I first came to town, eighteen long years ago. And last year I saw him in town. He . . ." Sam reflected. "He told me to go see Magowin. I was on my way to see you . . ."

"He's a reserved man, this Menro." Geoffrey smiled. "Rarely in town, you know. He appeared to me to be a man of moderate means. He would stop in to make payments on loans for others, several accounts at one time. I assumed, of course, that he was serving as agent in some way—perhaps a middleman of sorts—another lender for those times when a mortgage payment could not be met. I dismissed him, for the most part, until I learned that he wasn't a middleman at all. I learned that he was helping folks all around this end of the realm to meet their financial obligations. I thought he must be a benevolent, foolish man who was charitably paying off the loans. When he arrived one day, I couldn't help but inquire of his motive in using his own money to pay the loans of others. His reply stunned me. He said this wasn't his own money, that the money had, indeed, come from the borrowers. He met with them twice a month as a group, held discussions, and then collected their moneys to bring to me—for their convenience. They were his students, he said. He was teaching them the way to prosperity—teaching them of budgeting and saving and investing—guiding them to be disciplined in paying their debts. Many had taken second jobs, he said. Some had sold possessions. But all were determined to honor their obligations, even to turning over their collateral if necessary.

"'But why do you do this?' I asked of him. He responded, 'Because I love them and God loves them and they are in need of help. These honest souls are now some of the wealthiest in town. They will bless this town beyond measure.'

"This is what he told me. I stared at the man—this Menro fellow. I couldn't help but say, 'These people are not wealthy. They live in modest homes and eke out livings in the market. Menro, I am one of the wealthiest men in the shire and not one of these people has one twentieth of my assets.'

"But he said directly to me, 'No, Geoffrey. You are one of the poorest men in town. Your heart is empty.' I should have laughed at him and sent him back to his so-called students, but I didn't. He spoke to me with such compassion, genuine concern, and sincere knowledge that I . . . well, I asked him what he meant. . . . And I don't need to tell you more, eh? You know exactly what he meant."

Sam listened, astonished. "You changed from this one conversation?"

Geoffrey chuckled again. "My, my, no. Heavens, no. For a full year Menro talked with me—every time he brought payments. I also came to know Magowin and Pastor Wright through Menro—men I knew in town, of course, but never as friends—certainly never as advisers. Slowly my soul allowed my heart to listen. Then my mind listened. But I was a hard case, eh? To be convinced that my talent was a gift to be used to serve others? To understand that God had a plan for my life and my knowledge all along? To realize that I was wasting precious time and precious money by serving only myself? How could I do all this?

"I must tell you, Sam, that I have faith that all who are willing to step into the Light and follow a divinely lit path can truly find glorious prosperity and meaning in life. For no one knows more than I how difficult it is to start over at the very first law—to put his life into God's hands—and to find and face the resounding truth in each law, one at a time. For you see, my God-given gifts serve the seventh—the very last law—and yet I could not possibly put them to proper use until I took each step toward understanding the whole. I walk with God now, Sam. I am no longer the man I was.

"Now I'm here to serve you. And you have something of great value, which is in need of preservation and stewardship. Ignore this and you ignore the seventh law—the Law of Preservation."

"So. . . ." Sam approached this information cautiously. "You still lend money and invest?"

"Of course. That is my profession—my service. My talent was not the source of my emptiness. Only my motive—greed for money. Now I use my gift to offer only fair, sound investment advice. Now I only invest in what truly warrants support—ventures that are undertaken with good intentions to create a business that serves the new owner and serves others. Now I charge the lowest interest rates in town and lend only to those who truly qualify—if I think the borrower will have difficulty meeting his payments, I don't disservice him by enabling him to be in debt. I look at each request—and most are for homes or carriages—and decide if each loan is good for the person who's asking. I turn many more down than I accept. The interest I earn goes back into the fund that helps others to open businesses or buy their homes. It is a circle of money that creates growth. The money itself is put to work. With my profits, I do as you do. I give generously, I save, and I budget. Since my stored savings are adequate for any emergency or short-term need, I continue to invest in several markets and several projects. I do not earn as much as I once did, but I do have great wealth that I'm nurturing and preserving. I have exciting plans for this source of financial energy."

Sam noticed that Geoffrey's eyes were twinkling. "You speak of the seventh law. I kept waiting for Magowin to wave me into his shop, or for Pastor Wright to present it to me. . . ."

"You are ready to implement it, and I would be honored to guide you through its principles."

Sam took a deep breath. "What is this final law?"

"It is this. Listen and understand. You cannot achieve highest prosperity until you understand and undertake the important work of preservation—in all areas of your life, including your finances. You must value and preserve your health, your relationships, those things in your community that add to the well-being of all, the integrity of your profession, the beauty and resources of God's earth, and your beliefs and traditions. Anything of great value that you do not work to preserve will slowly pass away—leaving very little behind for those who follow you. The seventh law is the Law of Preservation. It is this law that calls for preserving the power and usefulness of your money—investing it.

"Money that is stored can serve one purpose only—as a short-term source for immediate, unexpected needs. Money that is stored is simply that—stored. It is not truly preserved, for it very slowly loses value over time, yes? Therefore, storing money beyond that which you might need in the short term is poor use and poor stewardship of that money. It only serves your hoarding instincts, which stem from fear. It serves no one else—not even your dreams. It serves no new businesses waiting to blossom. It serves no research projects. It stagnates the flow of money, and it stunts your future possibilities, capabilities, and generosity.

"This law directs that we take very seriously the money in our care—that we preserve it. Not sit on it, not foolishly gamble with it, but faithfully, wisely place it into investments that will allow it to flourish and grow. In this way we keep it actively involved—we allow it to work. You can ignore this law, dismissing investments as mere greedy ventures, and possibly have a hundred thousand gold pieces when you reach your older years. Or you can apply this law and have three hundred thousand pieces—which you can leave to your children . . . or donate to charity if you are so inclined . . . or fund your next dream—for you will never stop dreaming, Sam."

"But I know nothing of investments. . . ."

"You will learn in time. You will become quite used to tracking and managing your investments. But to start, you really need very little."

"What do I need?"

Geoffrey smiled broadly. "You will need a surplus of savings in the bank—which you have. You will need to set a time when both you and Suzette can meet with an adviser. And then you will need that adviser . . . which you have, if you accept my guidance."

"Yes, indeed! We will meet with you soon! This is actually quite exciting, isn't it? I will become an investor—a counseled investor, this time! Just like a wealthy man!"

"You are a wealthy man, Sam. A very wealthy man. But, here, before you go home to speak with Suzette, please let us finish this tea. After all," Geoffrey added with a wink, "it cost me seventeen farthings a pound!"

. . .

"Magowin, you look as though you married a fine cook!" Sam stepped into the cobbler's shop and hugged his old teacher.

"Ho-ho, my friend! You have a mischievous look in your

eye. What have you been up to—a discussion with Pastor Wright? Oh . . . wait. . . . You haven't come to recite fancy poetry to me, have you?" Magowin stepped back and peered over his spectacles at Sam.

"I'll leave that to Pastor Wright," laughed Sam. "No, I have not come from the parsonage. I have just come from Geoffrey's."

"Ah, my soft-spoken friend . . . he forgets that I am hard of hearing, but I love him just the same."

"He is soft-spoken, but I heard every word he said to me. He is to counsel Suzette and me in setting up our first investments with our surplus savings!"

"Ha! A fellow preservationist!" Magowin's merry face broke into a wide, exuberant smile as he clapped Sam on the back. "You will do fine! You will truly enjoy watching your money grow! But there is much more to this seventh law than preserving your money, you know this, yes?"

"I think so . . ." started Sam.

"In time, in time—God will let you know. Follow your heart and then you will know what you are called upon to leave for the next generations."

"Such grand words, Magowin! Surely a man such as I—"

"A man such as you . . ." Magowin looked at Sam with great affection. "A man such as you can make a trail that brings hope to so many—you must have faith, Sam. You must have faith."

. . .

"Sam, I have wonderful news!" exclaimed Suzette as Sam skipped through the door.

"I have news also," announced Sam breathlessly, "but I'll listen to you first. What is this news?"

"I have found an apprentice!"

Sam paused. "An apprentice?"

"Yes, Sam. I've been praying and praying that the right person would come along. Her mother and father run the mill at the northern bend of the river."

"I know of them. Fine people. And this girl . . . ?"

"Netta. She's only thirteen, Sam, but her mother showed me her embroidery work, and it . . . it brought tears to my eyes. Every detail . . . the designs . . . at such a young age. . . ." Suzette stopped to calm her excitement. "And she wants to learn from me, Sam. Her mother came to ask if I would be willing to take on an apprentice. I hesitated at first, but then she showed me her work and I knew that my prayers had been answered."

"You have been praying about this? And you say that *I* keep secrets!" Sam smiled and hugged his overjoyed wife.

"I know, Sam, but we've both been so busy, and this wish—this dream I have to pass on my ideas and the love and respect I have for my craft. . . . I—I could scarcely utter it to myself, I wished it so much. As much as I have hoped it so, I don't think our daughters will carry on this work. They will all be fine seamstresses, to be sure, but this is not their passion. Martha is a teacher—I know this. Lizzie lives to be outside in the garden watching things grow, and Mary . . . Mary is a thinker. I'm not sure what God has planned for her, but she will help others in some way with her reasoning skills. You know how I feel about the quality and love that goes into what I create. And now . . . now I will train a young woman who has great talent. I will share with her my ideas and my beliefs—and the need to add love to that talent. This work I do . . . this small bit of work that I have chosen in life . . . it will be carried on. It will be carried on!" Suzette's eyes glistened.

Sam listened, understanding, smiling. "This is indeed wonderful news."

"But, Sam, this will mean that, at first, I'll profit less. I must pay Netta some wages—not much, but some—and I'll be spending time teaching her. That will slow down my own work, and it will be a while before I can assign actual commissions to her. But in time, I'll actually be able to take many more orders and, together, Netta and I will be able to build this business. She will learn everything—the books, the customers, the purchasing. . . . Oh, Sam, I have envisioned this for so long!"

"Think nothing of the money, Suzette. We've managed on less, so we know that we can accomplish anything! Plus I am earning more now and have brighter prospects. This is a worthy undertaking—and I have complete faith in your decisions and dreams. God is smiling and you will be blessed by this."

"So many plans to make! I must prepare an area for Netta . . . such a small room . . . but we will make do. . . . Oh, Sam—you said you also have something to tell me! Forgive me. What is your news?"

"Well, it's not as exciting as your news, but . . . Geoffrey has asked that we sit down with him and plan out how we will be investing our savings."

Suzette stared at Sam. "Investing? Oh, Sam. I'm not sure we should risk putting any of our savings into investments. What if we lose money? Can't we just keep things as they are?"

"Then it will never grow, Suzette. This won't be like the last time. I won't invest in risky ventures. I now have more respect for our money than that. But we do need to put it to work. We've got to, or it will sit in a bank, benefiting no one—not even us. We won't choose any investments that we both don't agree on. And Geoffrey will help us. He'll advise us."

"Geoffrey? But he's in the business of lending money to people in need! Why should we trust him to work toward our staying *out* of debt?"

Sam smiled, then explained all that Geoffrey had related.

Suzette listened, and finally said quietly, "First let us pray and give thanks to God for these new blessings. Then let us decide when to go see Geoffrey."

. . .

With Geoffrey's guidance, Sam and Suzette's money began to take part in the commerce of their town, their shire, and throughout the realm.

They kept 3,600 gold pieces in the bank—enough to cover six-month's worth of necessities, as Geoffrey advised. The remaining 400 they placed with Geoffrey to go into four different investments—after a long session of questions, answers, and instructions.

"Why four?" Suzette had asked.

"Would you want to rely on orders from only one customer all year, Suzette?"

"Oh, no. Of course not. I need a range of customers to ensure that I have steady work."

"Ah . . . the same is true here. There will be times when one market or one fund of money is less profitable, but the others will be profiting greatly. You serve your money well by allowing it to take part in a variety of markets. Diversity is the key to being at peace with your investments."

Sam and Suzette learned that there was a wide variety of options—with varying degrees of risk and earnings potential. "This one fund that I recommend to you," Geoffrey noted, "the one invested in grocers around the shire—this goes up in value more slowly than the others, but every three months it will pay you a dividend—a small share of the profits—much like receiving interest from the bank."

"Wonderful!" exclaimed Sam and Suzette. "So, we will have income from this?"

Geoffrey put up his hand. "Yes, but the wise plan is to ask that this small dividend be reinvested into more stock. This way you earn dividends on your dividends—your earnings are compounded, and your overall return is higher. Plus"—Geoffrey smiled—"it is the disciplined way to approach these dividends. Until you need income from your investments, why not instead put them back to work for you?"

And so they did. Every week they continued to put 20 percent of their earnings into the bank, for emergencies and unexpected bills. At the end of each month they left 3,600 gold pieces in the bank and took the surplus to Geoffrey to invest into their four accounts. Every three months their dividends were reinvested. And slowly, slowly their money grew, building upon itself—and helping to support and build other businesses, services, and new ideas.

. . .

And so it was that Sam rebuilt his life on a firm foundation with sound cornerstones and the highest quality building blocks. His earnings were not always the same each month, depending upon his contracts, but how he handled those earnings was always the same.

Suzette's income was less for quite a while after she took Netta under her wing, but her concern was not profits but growth and preservation of the integrity of her craft. She delighted in her new work—mentoring a young person to carry on her ethics and workmanship—investing in another so that together they could someday work in partnership to serve a broader base of customers.

Sam's commissions on building grew steadily as Grecco's faith in Sam grew more firm. The day came when Sam no longer worked as crewman between management jobs, because there were no "between-job" times. He was a full-time foreman once more, just as he had been not two short years before. After several years of handling larger and more prestigious projects, Grecco chose Sam to head his entire guild operations, thereby placing him over every foreman and every project. Sam's organizational and budgeting skills, his ingenuity and foresight, and his management style made him a wise and enthusiastic leader. But it was his heart, his dedication to God, and his sincere love for the people of the town and his crews that commanded respect and dedication from all who worked with him.

The realm and the town were flourishing, so Sam and Suzette's investments grew and flowed throughout the commercial community. Their lifestyle never reflected the great wealth that was growing under their care. Yet, when storms devastated a poor section of town, Sam and Suzette gladly donated money to help rebuild it—and oh, what a blessing to be able to do so. When Netta's father suffered a severe accident, Sam and Suzette sent for the finest physician and paid the bill and oh, what a blessing to be able to do so. When Martha expressed her desire to attend the women's teaching school in the next town, Sam and Suzette had the resources to pay the tuition, her weekly room and board, and her transportation on the weekends—and oh, what a wonderful blessing to be able to do so.

Despite their successes, Sam and Suzette chose to remain in their cozy home. By building on two extra rooms (which delighted their daughters) they created a truly comfortable, warm place with lovely things to lift their spirits and fine books and food to feed their souls and bodies. Sam had never felt so fortunate—or so prosperous—in all his life!

. . .

The day came when the King decreed that he was looking for a wise and steady mind who could form a planning commission to steer the development of the many growing towns in the kingdom.

"I want a man who adheres to the wisdom of God!" announced the King.

"We know such a man," said the church leaders.

"I want a man who can set and stick to priorities!" announced the King.

"We know such a man," said the teachers.

"I want a man whose motive is genuine concern for my people and who will not influence decisions to line his own pockets!" announced the King.

"We know such a man," said the laborers.

"I want a man who has generously given of himself to others!" announced the King.

"We know such a man," said the widows.

"I want a man who knows not just how to study but how to understand!" announced the King.

"We know such a man," said the town council members.

"I want a man who is adept at planning and budgeting, a man who avoids debt and lavish spending!" declared the King.

"We know such a man," said the trade guild members.

"I want a man who will preserve what is good in these towns, who knows the value of investment, and who considers the future while planning today's course!" announced the King.

"I know such a man," said Geoffrey, meeting privately with the King.

"Bring him to me," announced the King.

. . .

Thus it came to be that a wood gatherer from the forest was placed in charge of gathering the best and brightest thinkers, planners, and builders in all the realm—to set a course for their growing communities. Under Sam's prudent guidance, an overall plan for the entire kingdom was laid out. Bridges, aqueducts, market areas, and roads were repaired, rebuilt, or newly constructed. Parks and forests were set aside to be preserved. Areas for farming and for market activities were established according to terrain, irrigation, and accessibility. Several towns combined their efforts on similar projects for the first time—a revolutionary idea that saved money and reduced the taxes of every citizen.

Sam appointed Marcus as a liaison to the King, to work out new ideas to promote citizen involvement and investment in their communities. These new ideas became positive laws. Those who donated to the building of schools and churches paid less tax. Those who had a poor year growing crops but who needed seed would pay a lower tax on their earnings. Those who agreed to assist and train the handicapped and underskilled—so that those overlooked citizens gained employment and became part of their towns' prosperity—were paid a salary out of those new workers' taxes.

Sam did not make every decision, but he did gather the minds that could build together—with integrity and vision. From a variety of professionals, from a variety of inventive thinkers and spiritual teachers, from a variety of laborers, from mothers and fathers, from young adults, and from the elderly he constructed a cohesive series of town plans that served the needs of all the townspeople. And the towns prospered. And the people prospered. And Sam knew that he had reached the pinnacle of all that he had been destined to achieve and offer in this life of his . . .

until one day . . .

. . . when a silver-haired gentleman, wearing a green woolen coat, came to see Sam in his office in the new town hall.

"I have come because I am a concerned citizen," he told Sam.

"What concerns you? How can I help?" replied Sam, standing to greet him.

"I am concerned that we have a resource that has been decreasing in value for generations. A valuable component of our kingdom has yet to become part of the prosperity available to all. We must preserve and invest in this neglected resource, or we will all be the poorer, I assure you."

Sam listened intently. Then, slowly, he spoke with great respect for the man he recognized before him. "Menro, it is you. Two times you have spoken wisely to me. Over twenty years ago, you made me realize I had not been offering the very best firewood—or my very best work. Ten years ago you directed me to a shoe cobbler to set my feet on the right path. Tell me what you speak of now, for I trust your judgment."

"I speak of our brothers and sisters deep in the forest."

Sam was silent for a long time. Finally he sat down, a bit wearily. "I know of these people, Menro. Often I have thought of them. My own parents have long since passed on, but there are many who come into my mind from time to time."

Then Sam looked up at this refined gentleman. With sorrow and regret he added, "And yours is a noble heart to consider them. But I must tell you that they care nothing for our carriage roads, brick buildings, aqueducts, and parks. They are resigned to their lot and they always will be. As long as they consider themselves better than the town beggars, they will be proud of their poverty. I know their ways and their thoughts. They will not come to join us in the town, I assure you, to take part in our prosperity. They have no money to invest, no dreams . . . and no hope. They have no love for us, Menro."

Undeterred, Menro spoke with quiet authority. "It makes no difference that they have no love for us. For you see, God has love for them. If they do not care for our great buildings, so be it. Let us clear a wide path and make a paved trail—a well-built trail that tells them they are worth the effort—that leads from our town to their village. Let us then send teachers and pastors to minister unto their hearts. God does not care if they have no money to invest. But he does care if we, who have so much, do not invest our resources and time in their souls.

"Perhaps you are right, Sam, and they will choose not to accept our fellowship. But perhaps there will be one child who learns to read and finds hope. Perhaps there will be one in pain who accepts medical help and finds hope. Perhaps there will be one young woman with a calling—with ideas that have been hushed—who welcomes the chance to talk to a pastor, and finds hope. And perhaps, Sam, there will be one young man who dreams of creating a better life as he collects his twigs and branches, who finds inspiration in your example—and finds hope. This is a building project that warrants action. It is a worthy investment. It is a worthy commission."

The heart of a simple wood gatherer heard these wise words and they resounded deep within him. He had lived an honorable, prosperous life. He had become a man of affluence and a man of influence. He had overseen the construction of great works and cultural centers. He had the respect of a King, wealth beyond his dreams, and he stood at the highest point of his career. And yet somehow he knew in that moment—with an elderly gentleman in a green woolen coat looking kindly into his eyes—that far greater work lay ahead. . . .

Sam stood up and shook Menro's hand. "Come, my friend. We have a trail to make."

7 Laws of Highest Prosperity

1. The Law of Wisdom
   Highest wisdom resides in God's supreme thought and love.

2. The Law of Priority
   Success that lasts can only be achieved when one prioritizes in accordance with divine instruction—at all levels, including financial matters.

3. The Law of Motive
   Meaningful work and living are motivated by unconditional love for others.

4. The Law of Generosity
   Service and giving create abundance, for others and ourselves.

5. The Law of Understanding
   To love with God's heart, see through His eyes, and think His thoughts are the ultimate goals for the truly enlightened spirit.

6. The Law of Preparation
   Being responsible with and wisely managing life resources requires commitment to truly important purpose and careful planning.

7. The Law of Preservation
   Wise stewardship ensures that money, principles, values, and spiritual guidance can be passed from one generation to the next.

About the Author

Cecil O. Kemp Jr. grew up on a small farm. He and Patty, his childhood sweetheart, have been married almost thirty years. Their two children are married and have given the Kemps four grandchildren.

In 1971, Cecil graduated college and began his professional career as a CPA working with one of the world's largest accounting firms. At twenty-three, he became chief financial officer of a public company and, before thirty, became its chief operating officer. From 1982–1998 the Kemps owned and operated many successful businesses. As a result of lessons learned from Cecil's near fatal accident in 1993 and introspection on his father's unexpected death in 1995, the Kemps sold all their businesses and have focused their energy full-time on writing, publishing, speaking, and retreat ministry.

Cecil's books offer wisdom and inspiration for the heart and hope for every season of life. In addition to *7 Laws of Highest Prosperity,* he is the author of four other inspirational paperbacks:

- *The Meeting Place: The Personal HeartSkill to Truly Make a Difference*
- *Success That Lasts: Living by the 7 Laws of Highest Prosperity in Modern Society*
- *Wisdom & Money: Applying the 7 Laws of Highest Prosperity to Make the Most of Your Money*
- *Wisdom Honor & Hope: The Inner Path to True Greatness*

He is also the creator of The Hope Collection, a series of beautiful, full-color gift books that are based on his concepts and writings. There are currently sixteen Hope Collection gift books:

- *A Book of Hope after Retirement: The Best Years Are Ahead*
- *A Book of Hope for a Better Life: Inspiration Today from Reflecting Back & Looking Within*
- *A Book of Hope for Achieving True Greatness: 26 Keys to Highest & Lasting Success*
- *A Book of Hope for Higher Connection: Truth, Inspiration & Wisdom for the Searching Soul*
- *A Book of Hope for Lasting Peace: Inspiring Thoughts for Possessing Real Hope & Security*
- *A Book of Hope for Leaders: 86 Day Guidebook to Leadership Greatness*
- *A Book of Hope for Loving Unconditionally: The Power & Passion for Living Life Fully*
- *A Book of Hope for Mothers: Celebrate the Joy of Children*
- *A Book of Hope for Parents: Inspiration & Wisdom for Successful Parenting*
- *A Book of Hope for Relationship Heartaches: Wisdom & Inspiration for Mending Broken Hearts*
- *A Book of Hope for Shaping a Life of Honor: How to Live a Life of True Excellence*
- *A Book of Hope for Students: Dream Big, Dream Wisely!*
- *A Book of Hope for the Storms of Life: Healing Words for Troubled Times*
- *A Book of Hope on Abiding Faith: Rediscovering the Rock of a Meaningful Life*
- *A Book of Hope on Prayer: Key to Successful Days, Lock of Secure Nights*
- *A Book of Hope we're Forgiven: The Healing Power of Forgiveness*

Our Approach to Writing and Publishing

The books of Cecil O. Kemp Jr. and The Wisdom Company challenge humanistic philosophies and conventional wisdom of modern culture.

The core value of loving, caring for, and focusing on God and others is featured in all the books. It is portrayed as the key to achieving true greatness, life, relationship, and leadership excellence and success that lasts.

Our books offer sound counsel and real hope based on the unchanging principles of eternal truth that are embedded in a positive and powerful message that comforts, encourages, heals, instructs, and inspires.

We value what is important in the here and now and eternity for individuals and the relationship, family, and organization units upon which a caring society and culture rest. Thus, we point readers first to spiritual reconciliation, renewal, and restoration, then to selflessness in daily living and working.

We are humbled to have the God-given call, privilege, honor, skills, and resources to produce works of literary distinction that focus on traditional values and contribute an extremely valuable perspective on the genuinely great issues of modern life.

We are proud that our books not only offer a view through the eternal scope and practical, sound solutions that stand the test of time but openly fly in the face of materialism, intellectualism, man-made religion, and all hot-air, empty humanistic philosophies that mostly create problems.

In promoting the values and priorities of eternal truth that run counter to popular culture, we produce books that are suited for a broad audience—readers of all ages in all places in the world who are open-minded and sincerely searching for the better way of living and working that begins with right relationship with God, a pure heart and Godlike character.